Farmer Boy

Written By: Laura Ingalls Wilder

Teacher Guide

Published by: Memoria Press
www.memoriapress.com

© 2010 by Memoria Press Copyright
All rights reserved
ISBN: 978-1-61538-046-6

Contributing Editors: Leigh Lowe, Brenda Janke, Anne Parry, Brittany Mann
Cover Illustration by Starr Steinbach
Cover & Layout Design by Karah J. Force

Contents

Farmer Boy

Appendix   83

Discussion Questions Key   93

Quizzes & Final Test   107

PREPARING TO READ:

REVIEW

- Orally review any previous vocabulary.
- Review the plot of the book as read so far.
- Periodically review the concepts of character, setting, and plot.

STUDY GUIDE PREVIEW

- Reading Notes:
  - Read aloud together
  - This section gives the student key characters, places, terms that are relevant to a particular time period, etc.
- Vocabulary:
  - Read aloud together so that students will recognize words when they come across them in their reading.
- Comprehension Questions:
  - Read through these questions with students to encourage purposeful reading.

READING:

- Student reads the chapter (or selection of the chapter for that lesson) independently or to the teacher (for younger students).
- For younger students, you can alternate between teacher-read and student-read passages. Model good reading skills. Encourage students to read expressively and smoothly. Teacher may occasionally take oral reading grades.
- While reading, mark each vocabulary word as you come across it.
- Have students take note in their study guide margin of pages where a comprehension question is answered.

AFTER READING:

VOCABULARY
- Look at each word within the context that it is used, and help your student come up with the best synonym that defines the word. (Make sure it is a synonym the student knows the meaning of.)
- Record the word's meaning in the students' study guides. (Use students' knowledge of Latin and other vocabulary to decipher meanings.)

COMPREHENSION QUESTIONS
- Older students can answer these questions independently, but younger students (2nd-4th) need to answer the questions orally, form a good sentence, and then write it down, using correct punctuation, capitalization, and spelling. (You may want to write the sentence down for the younger student after forming it orally, and then let the student copy it perfectly.)
- It is not necessary to write the answer to every question. Some may be better answered orally.
- Answering questions and composing answers is a valuable learning activity. Questions require students to think; writing a concise answer is a good composition exercise.

QUOTATIONS AND DISCUSSION QUESTIONS
- Use the Quotations and Discussion Questions section of each lesson as a guide to your oral discussion of the key concepts in the chapter that may not be covered in the comprehension questions.
- These talking points can take your oral discussion to a higher level than covered in the students' written work. Use this time as an opportunity to introduce higher-level thinking. You can introduce concepts the students may not be mature enough to fully understand yet but that would be beneficial for them to begin thinking about.
- A key to the Discussion Questions is in the back of the Teacher Guide.

ENRICHMENT
- The Enrichment activities include composition, copywork, dictation, research, mapping, drawing, poetry work, literary terms, and more.
- This section has a variety of activities in it, but the most valuable activity is composition. Your student should complete at least one composition assignment each week. Proof student's work and have student copy composition until grammatically perfect. Insist on clear, concise writing. For younger students, start with 2-3 sentences, and do the assignment together. The student can form good sentences orally as you write them down, and then the student copies them.
- These activities can be completed as time and interest allow. Do not feel you need to complete all of these activities. Choose the ones that you feel are the best use of your students' time.

UNIT REVIEW AND TESTS
- There is a unit review and a quiz or test following every few lessons (varies by individual guide).
- On the weeks that have these reviews and tests, you may want to do the review early in the week, and then drill it orally a couple of times before giving the test at the end of the week.
- A final comprehensive test is also included.

Teaching Guidelines

Reading Notes

waist	the upper part of a garment, extending from the shoulders to the waistline
moccasins	soft leather slippers
primer	an elementary textbook for teaching children to read
jeering	mocking; taunting

Vocabulary

1. a little boy **trudged** to school _____walked with heavy feet_____

2. Five big boys were **scuffling** in the deep snow by the path. _wrestling_____

3. They **boasted** that no teacher could finish the winter term __bragged_____

4. Mr. Corse **rapped** on his desk with his ruler_____knocked_____

5. No whispering was permitted in school, and no **fidgeting**. _moving restlessly_____

Comprehension Questions

1. Give the names and ages of the four Wilder children. _____The Wilder children are Royal (13),_ Eliza Jane (12), Alice (10), and Almanzo (8)._____

2. Briefly describe Eliza Jane. __She is bossy. She always knows what is best to do but makes_ Almanzo and Alice do it._____

3. Why does Almanzo have to be the one to carry the dinner-pail to school? _____ He is the youngest in the family._____

4. Who is the teacher and why is he staying with the Wilder family at their home? _____ Mr. Corse is the teacher. Each family boards the teacher for two weeks during the school year, and it is the Wilders' turn to host him._____

5. Find where Mr. Corse is described and list three characteristics that describe him.____Pg. 5___ Mr. Corse is slim, pale, young, patient, and gentle._____

6. In what way are students punished for not knowing their lessons?_____Royal's hand was_ spanked with a ruler. Almanzo has to stay in from recess to study._____

Quotations

No whispering was permitted in school, and no fidgeting. Everyone must be perfectly still and keep his eyes fixed on his lesson. Almanzo and Miles held up their primers and tried not to swing their legs. Their legs grew so tired that they ached, dangling from the edge of the seat.

But Mr. Corse never beat a little boy's hand with his ruler. When Almanzo could not spell a word, Mr. Corse said: "Stay in at recess and learn it."

Discussion Questions

1. *Find the title page of the book, then turn the page to see publishing information. In what year did Laura Ingalls Wilder write *Farmer Boy*? Based on this knowledge and the first paragraph of the chapter, figure out the year in which the story is set. Where does the story take place?

2. Locate New York state on a U.S. map. What would the weather be like in that part of the country?

3. Why does Mr. Corse give the Hardscrabble boys another chance after they are tardy?

4. Explain the seating arrangement in the classroom. What do you think is the purpose of this arrangement?

*Discussion questions that have a * are NECESSARY to discuss with students, as they may appear on a test and are generally important in understanding the full flavor of the story.

Enrichment

Focus Passage: Copy the second paragraph beginning on page 1 ("Down a long road … nine years old"). Spelling, punctuation, and capitalization should be perfect.

Down a long road through the woods a little boy trudged to school, with his big brother Royal and his two sisters, Eliza Jane and Alice. Royal was thirteen years old, Eliza Jane was twelve, and Alice was ten. Almanzo was the youngest of all, and this was his first going-to-school, because he was not quite nine years old.

Reading Notes

eave	the part of a roof that extends out past the wall
fringe	a decorative border or edging of hanging threads attached to a band
haymow	the part of a barn where hay or straw is stored
hoopskirt	a long full skirt belled out with a series of connected circular supports

Vocabulary

1. The wise, sedate work-horses **placidly** munched hay. _____ calmly, peacefully _____

2. But the colts ran about excited, on their **gangling** legs _____ awkwardly tall, long-limbed _____

3. a plate of **quivering** headcheese _____ trembling _____

4. Almanzo ate the sweet, **mellow** baked beans. _____ pleasant, subtle _____

5. He **demolished** a tall heap of pale mashed turnips _____ destroyed _____

Comprehension Questions

1. What chores does Almanzo do after school? How are they different from the chores his sisters does? _____ Almanzo's chores include cleaning stalls, feeding hay to the animals, milking cows, and feeding the barn cats. His sisters work in the house, cooking and cleaning, with their mother. _____

2. Contrast the old work-horses with the young colts. _____ Old horses are calm (experienced and content); young horses are frisky (inquisitive and ready for work). _____

3. Describe Mother. _____ Mother is short, plump, and pretty. She keeps very busy taking care of the house and the meals. _____

4. Who gets served a plate of food first? Who gets served last? Why? _____ Mr. Corse (because he is a guest) is served first; Almanzo (because he is youngest) eats last. _____

5. Why can't Almanzo speak at the table? _____ The rule at table is: "Children must be seen and not heard." _____

Quotations

Father was an important man. He had a good farm. He drove the best horses in that country. His word was as good as his bond, and every year he put money in the bank. When Father drove into Malone, all the townspeople spoke to him respectfully.

The cold was cruel. The night was black and still, and the stars were tiny sparkles in the sky. Almanzo was glad to get into the big kitchen, warm with fire and candle-light. He was very hungry.

Discussion Questions

1. *The first quote above describes Father. According to it and other statements in the chapter, what kind of a man is he? What does the author mean by saying, "His word was as good as his bond"? From this chapter, how can you tell he is a good father to his children?

2. *Why doesn't Father trust Almanzo around the colts? What does he fear will happen, and how does Almanzo feel about this?

3. In the second quote above, the cold is described as being cruel. What does that mean? How does that phrase help you understand how Almanzo is feeling at that moment?

Enrichment

The author describes the Wilders' barnyard in great detail. When a story includes considerable descriptions like these, it is helpful to draw a picture of what it might look like. It can then be used later for reference and clarity.

Draw a simple map of the Wilder barnyard below. Label each barn and what it is used for.
(*Suggestion: begin with a small compass star in a corner. Use a pencil so you can erase if necessary.*)

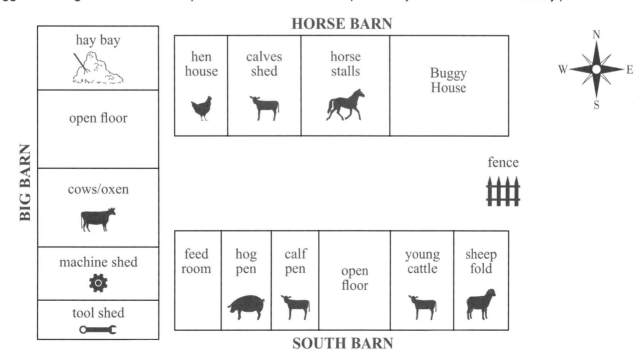

Reading Notes

embroidery   a design sewn on cloth as a decoration

dampers   a movable plate in a fireplace used to regulate the draft

bureau   a piece of furniture; dresser

Vocabulary

1. Mother and the girls washed the dishes and swept the **pantry** _area for food storage_

2. Mother **banked** the kitchen fire with ashes for the night _piled coals to keep them hot_

3. he broke the **charred** logs into a shimmering bed of coals. _partially burned_

4. He ran **clattering** upstairs. _noisily_

5. Father was **rousing** up the young cattle. _waking_

Comprehension Questions

1. What are the Wilder family bedtime snacks? What do they do for entertainment at night? _____

   They eat popcorn, apples, and cider. They sit around the warm stove, and each work on their own

   project while listening to Eliza Jane read from the newspaper.

2. What does popcorn make Almanzo think of? _He thinks of Indians, Pilgrims, and Thanksgiving;_

   he also thinks about eating popcorn and milk.

3. Why does father get up at night to exercise the young cattle? _____

   If they lay still on such a cold night, they could freeze in their sleep, so Father exercises them to

   warm them up and prevent them from freezing.

4. Why does Almanzo dread going to school? _____

   He doesn't want to see the big mean boys from Hardscrabble Settlement thrash Mr. Corse.

Quotations

They all settled down cosily by the big stove in the dining-room wall. … Mother knitted and rocked in her high-backed rocking-chair. Father carefully scraped a new ax-handle with a bit of broken glass. Royal carved a chain of tiny links from a smooth stick of pine, and Alice sat on her hassock, doing her woolwork embroidery. And they all ate popcorn and apples, and drank sweet cider, except Eliza Jane. Eliza Jane read aloud the news in the New York weekly paper. Almanzo sat on a footstool by the stove … He thought about popcorn.

Discussion Questions

1. What chores does the family do immediately after supper?

2. Find the pages that describe the Wilders' breakfast. What do they eat? Why do you think Mother cooks so much variety for this meal?

Enrichment

Learn More: The words below are unique to the setting of *Farmer Boy*.

Find the meaning of the words or phrases to learn more about how the Wilders lived. Write a short definition that explains or describes each.

parlor: _____ a room used mostly for entertaining company _____

dinner-pail: _____ a covered bucket in which the children carried their lunch to school _____

pannikin: _____ a small pan or metal cup _____

tallow: _____ fat obtained from cattle, sheep, or horses and used to make candles, soap, etc. ___

cellar: _____ an underground basement area used for storage because it is cool _____

hassock: _____ a thick cushion used as a footstool _____

goose-feather bed: _____ a mattress stuffed with goose feathers _____

headcheese: _____ a jellied loaf made from chopped and boiled parts of a hog's feet and head ___

Reading Notes

trustees   members of a board elected to make important decisions for an organization
lick   to fight and defeat
bested   defeated

Vocabulary

1. they all grinned **impudently** at Mr. Corse. _____ disrespectfully _____
2. they went in **soberly** and **soberly** sat down. _____ seriously _____
3. The big boys came ... **jostling** one another. _____ pushing or shoving _____
4. Big Bill Ritchie **swaggered** in. _____ walked pridefully _____
5. He **blubbered** and begged. _____ sobbed noisily _____

Comprehension Questions

1. Describe Mr. Ritchie. Why is he proud of his son, Big Bill Ritchie? _____ Mr. Ritchie is a _____ big, rough man with a loud voice. He is proud that Bill can thrash the teacher and break up the schoolhouse and thinks it is a funny joke. _____

2. Why don't the students know their lessons on this day? _____
   The students are worried about their teacher. They are too frightened and distracted to concentrate.

3. What makes Big Bill's gang change their attitude? _____ When the other boys see how Mr. Corse defeats Bill, they flee in fear. _____

4. Describe the surprising events that occur at school. _____
   Big Bill and his gang threaten the teacher, but Mr. Corse surprises and defeats them with a bullwhip.

5. What news does Almanzo overhear while his father and Mr. Corse are talking? _____
   Almanzo learns that the bullwhip belongs to his father who had loaned it to Mr. Corse.

Lesson 4: Surprise

Quotations

"That's his business. When a man undertakes a job, he has to stick to it till he finishes it. If Corse is the man I think he is, he'd thank nobody for interfering."

Who said this? <u>Father</u>

About whom? <u>the school teacher, Mr. Corse</u>

Discussion Questions

1. *In the quote above, what is Father saying about Mr. Corse?

2. Why does Mr. Corse focus on Big Bill instead of dealing with any of the other big boys first?

3. What virtues does Mr. Corse display in the way he disciplines Big Bill?

Enrichment

Focus Passage: Look at the last full paragraph on page 40, beginning with "That's his business ..." Copy the entire paragraph *directly* from the book. Spelling, punctuation, and capitalization should be perfect.

"That's his business," said Father. "When a man undertakes a job, he has to stick to it till he finishes it. If Corse is the man I think he is, he'd thank nobody for interfering."

Reading Notes

yoke	a crossbar with two U-shaped pieces that encircle the necks of a pair of animals working together
"break" the calves	to train to obey; to tame
shingle	a thin, oblong piece of material, such as wood, laid in overlapping rows to cover the roof of a building
treadle	a pedal or lever operated by the foot
stanchion	a framework of vertical bars, used to secure cattle in a stall

Vocabulary

1. Their little red sides were **sleek** and silky _____ smooth; slick _____

2. they stared **innocently** at him. _____ without knowledge _____

3. but of course he could not **contradict** Father. _____ to speak against _____

4. Calves will get **sullen** and stop minding you _____ moody _____

5. and **daintily** pawed with their slender legs and little hoofs _____ delicately _____

Comprehension Questions

1. Why does Almanzo not have to go to school on his birthday? _____ He does not have to go when there are "more important things to do," such as training his calves to behave like oxen. _____

2. What is Almanzo's first birthday present? _____ His father has made a small yoke for his calves. _____

3. Why does Almanzo feel as if the whole morning has gone by in only a moment? _____
He was so busy working with his calves that he lost track of time.

4. Why is Almanzo allowed to train his calves but not Father's colts? _____
His father says training colts is a man's job because one has to be very experienced. One mistake could ruin the colt.

5. How does Mother surprise Almanzo? She tells him to get wood from the woodshed to fill the woodbox in the kitchen. There he finds his second present, a sled.

Quotations

"Well, son, I'll leave you to figure it out." And he went into the barn.

Who said this? __Father__   To whom? __Almanzo__

"Whose sled is that, Father? Is it—it isn't for me?" Mother laughed and Father twinkled his eyes and asked, "Do you know any other nine-year-old that wants it?"

Discussion Questions

1. *Read the first quote above. The book says Almanzo feels he is now old enough to do important things by himself. Why? Why do you think Father stops helping him and goes into the barn?

2. Explain how Almanzo teaches Star and Bright to understand "Giddap" and "Whoa."

3. While Almanzo is watching Mother work, she tells him she is making a suit for Royal that he will need next winter. Why will it take her so long to make this suit?

4. Compare and contrast Almanzo's birthday with your own birthday celebration.

Enrichment

Focus Passage: Look at the fifth paragraph on page 50 beginning with "Almanzo did not ..." Copy the entire paragraph *directly* from the book. Spelling, punctuation, and capitalization should be perfect.

Almanzo did not go to school that day. He did not have to go to school when there were more important things to do. He carried the little yoke to the barn, and Father went with him. Almanzo thought that if he handled the calves perfectly, perhaps Father might let him help with the colts next year.

Reading Notes

bobsled	a long sled made of two shorter sleds joined together, one behind the other
plaid	cloth with a checked pattern
laprobe	a blanket or fur piece used to cover the lap, legs, and feet

Vocabulary

1. The horses trotted **briskly** _____ <u>quickly; with spirit</u>

2. A sharp wind blew there, driving **wisps** of snow before it. _____ <u>thin fragments</u>

3. He felt himself falling **headlong** into the dark water. _____ <u>head first</u>

4. leaving them to fill every **crevice** tightly with sawdust _____ <u>crack</u>

5. and handed him the pitcher of sweetened cream **speckled** with nutmeg. <u>sprinkled</u>

Comprehension Questions

1. What type of weather was perfect for cutting ice? Why? <u>Extreme cold was perfect because</u> <u>when the blocks were lifted from the pond, no water would drip; the ice would freeze instantly.</u>

2. Who are Lazy John and French Joe? Compare them to the Wilder family. <u>Lazy John and</u> <u>French Joe are Frenchmen who sometimes work for Father. (While the Wilders plan ahead and</u> <u>work hard all the time, the Frenchmen live for today. They sacrifice some comforts and security to</u> <u>play, drink, and laugh.)</u>

3. Describe what happens when Almanzo gets too close to the edge of the hole. <u>Almanzo</u> <u>almost falls into the cold water, but French Joe grabs him just in time and saves him.</u>

4. How do the Wilders keep the ice frozen even in the summer months? <u>They stack the</u> <u>blocks and pack them in sawdust in the ice-house.</u>

5. How do Almanzo and Royal distract themselves until dinnertime? <u>Royal and Almanzo daydream</u> <u>about what they would like to eat best.</u>

Quotations

"You flipped that penny yet?" Everybody laughed but Almanzo. He did not know the joke.

Who said this? ___Father___   To whom? ___French Joe and Lazy John___

French Joe grabbed him just in time. He heard a shout and felt a rough hand jerk him by one leg, he felt a terrific crash, and then he was lying on his stomach on the good, solid ice. He got up on his feet. Father was coming, running.

Discussion Questions

1. Read the first quote. What is the punchline of the "flip a penny" joke? Why is it about Irishmen, not Frenchmen?

2. What would have happened if Almanzo had actually fallen in the ice?

3. Why do you think sawdust is used to cover the top layer of ice and to fill the cracks?

4. How do the Wilders use the ice they store in the summer months?

Enrichment

Sequencing: Describe the process of cutting ice and filling the ice house. Your sentences should be organized to show the correct order of the tasks. Be sure to write in complete sentences.

1. They chop a triangle in the ice to check its thickness. (20 inches)

2. They cut strips of ice 20 feet long by 20 inches wide.

3. They divide the strips into 20 inch blocks.

4. They load the blocks on the sled and place them in the ice-house 3 inches apart.

5. They fill and pack every crack with sawdust, also covering the top.

6. They repeat this process until the ice-house is filled to the roof.

Reading Notes

new-fangled	new type or style
muffler	a heavy scarf worn around the neck
Comanches	a Native American people formerly living in the southern Great Plains
rye'n'injun dough	a combination of rye and corn dough ("injun" - Indian)
drawers	thermal underwear pants

Vocabulary

1. Royal chopped at it, and when his **hatchet** went through _____ small short-handled ax

2. An **avalanche** of ice came down with a splintering crash. _____ snow or landslide

3. The noise was **immense**. _____ very large

4. Such a **racket** I never heard! _____ loud noise; clamor

5. pouring **scrolls** of molasses over all. _____ rolls or ribbon shapes

Comprehension Questions

1. What does Almanzo like best about Saturdays? What does he like least? Almanzo likes the fact
   that Saturday is baking day. He does not like taking a bath.

2. Why does Mother prepare Sunday dinner on Saturday night? _____
   It has to bake slowly for many hours.

3. What is the Saturday-night feeling? _____
   The feeling is of clean skin and clean clothes.

4. How does Mother determine whether or not Almanzo is clean? Why does she need to check him?
   She checks his ears and the back of his neck and looks at his face. He is young; he isn't attentive
   to the details and still needs a little help.

5. Why do the Wilders bathe only once a week on Saturday night? _____
   Getting everything ready for bathing is a big ordeal and takes a long time. They bathe on Saturday
   night because they want to look their best for church on Sunday.

Quotations

Almanzo liked baking-day. But he didn't like Saturday night. On Saturday night there was no cosy evening by the heater, with apples, popcorn, and cider. Saturday night was bath night.

He felt very clean and good, and his skin felt sleek in the fresh, warm clothes. It was the Saturday-night feeling.

Who is this referring to? __Almanzo__

Discussion Questions

1. How does Mother make doughnuts? What is special about her doughnuts?

2. The Wilders' bath procedure is involved. What other chores were more difficult then?

3. What bedtime clothing does Almanzo put on after his bath? Why must he dress so warmly?

Enrichment

Focus Passage: Reread the first quote above, then copy it on the lines below. Spelling, punctuation, and capitalization should be perfect.

Almanzo liked baking-day. But he didn't like Saturday night. On Saturday night there was no cosy

evening by the heater, with apples, popcorn, and cider. Saturday night was bath night.

Reading Notes

sleigh	a light vehicle mounted on runners for use on snow or ice, drawn by a horse
calico	light-weight, printed cotton fabric
basque	a woman's close-fitting bodice

Vocabulary

1. Mother … buttered it **lavishly** _____ generously; extravagantly

2. Oh dear me, my ribbons are **mussed**. _____ in disarray; out of order

3. Then they all walked **sedately** into the church. _____ calmly, in an unhurried manner

4. Father allowed him to brush and **currycomb** … the horses _____ grooming tool

5. The whole afternoon they sat in the **drowsy** warm dining-room. sleepy

Comprehension Questions

1. What are the three grades of cloth mentioned? Who wears each type? _____ Poor people wear homespun; Royal and Almanzo wear fullcloth; Father, Mother, and the girls wear store-bought cloth woven by machines.

2. Why do the Wilders travel to Malone? How far away is Malone? The Wilders go to Malone to go to church. The city is five miles away, but the trip takes at least half an hour by carriage.

3. Where does Almanzo's cousin Frank live? Why? Frank lives in the town of Malone because his father (Uncle Wesley) owns the potato-starch mill. They don't have a farm.

4. How does the Wilder family always spend their Sunday afternoons? Why? They sit quietly because Sunday is not a day for working or playing. It is a day of rest, a day for going to church and sitting still.

5. Why is Almanzo glad to do the chores Sunday evening? It is difficult for him to sit still all day. He is glad to have something active to do.

Quotations

Mother always flew. Her feet went pattering, her hands moved so fast you could hardly watch them. She never sat down in the daytime, except at her spinning-wheel or loom ... But on Sunday morning she made everybody else hurry, too.

But Almanzo just sat. He had to. He was not allowed to do anything else, for Sunday was not a day for working or playing. It was a day for going to church and for sitting still.

Discussion Questions

1. "Every man who belonged to the church paid rent for a shed, according to his means, and Father had the best one." What does the phrase "according to his means" mean? What does this say about Father?

2. *Farmer Boy* includes many detailed descriptions of food. Why do you think this is?

3. What are Almanzo's thoughts about his cousin Frank's "store-boughten" cap? Based on what Royal says, how does Almanzo know he wants a cap like that too?

4. Consider the way in which the Wilders traveled. Contrast the differences between their means of travel and how you travel.

Enrichment

Focus Passage: Copy from the second paragraph on page 94 beginning with "But Almanzo just sat ..." through the last paragraph of the chapter, ending with "... time to do the chores." Since you are beginning your copying in the middle of a paragraph, don't worry about indenting this time. Spelling, punctuation, and capitalization should be perfect.

But Almanzo just sat. He had to. He was not allowed to do anything else, for Sunday was not a day for

working or playing. It was a day for going to church and sitting still.

    Almanzo was glad when it was time to do the chores.

Reading Notes

whiplash   a flexible whip used to train oxen

auger   a hand tool used to drill holes in wood or ice

fraidy-cat   slang for a timid or fearful person

Vocabulary

1. They kicked up their heels and ran **bawling** around the barnyard _____crying_____

2. When the calves feel the **heft,** they're liable to run away. _____weight_____

3. When the calves feel the heft, they're **liable** to run away. _____likely_____

4. He spit it out, and **wallowed**, scrambled up. _____rolled_____

5. The yoke was crooked and their necks were **askew** in the bows. _____bent to one side_____

Comprehension Questions

1. How does Almanzo teach Star and Bright to turn right and left? _____He cracks the whip near the opposite side of their heads to teach them to turn away from it. At the same time, he gives commands—"gee" to turn left and "haw" to turn right._____

2. Why does Almanzo tell Father about his patience while training the oxen? _____He hopes that Father will be impressed with how patient he had become and allow him to currycomb the colts as a result. But Father doesn't seem to think of this._____

3. Who are the French boys? Who are their fathers? _____Pierre and Louis are the French boys. Pierre's father is Lazy John; Louis' father is French Joe._____

4. What is Almanzo's splendid idea concerning his calves? _____Almanzo decides to see if his team of calves can pull his sled with passengers on it because Star and Bright are behaving so well._____

5. What does Almanzo forget to teach Star and Bright? _____He has forgotten to teach them to obey his commands while he is riding behind them. He finds this out after his sled crashes._____

Quotations

He knew you could never teach an animal anything if you struck it, or even shouted at it angrily. He must always be gentle, and quiet, and patient, even when they made mistakes. Star and Bright must like him and trust him and know he would never hurt them, for if they were once afraid of him they would never be good, willing, hard-working oxen.

"I guess I know how to handle my own calves."

Who said this? <u>Almanzo</u>

Discussion Questions

1. Based on the first quote above, why does Almanzo not whip Star and Bright even when they are not obeying?

2. Read the second quote. Why does Almanzo say this? Judging from the outcome of his "splendid idea," do you agree with this statement? Why or why not?

Enrichment

Focus Passage: Copy the last paragraph on page 98 ("He knew you …") through the top of page 99 to the end of the paragraph ("… hard-working oxen."). Spelling, punctuation, and capitalization should be perfect.

He knew you could never teach an animal anything if you struck it, or even shouted at it angrily. He must always be gentle, and quiet, and patient, even when they made mistakes. Star and Bright must like him and trust him and know he would never hurt them, for if they were once afraid of him they would never be good, willing, hard-working oxen.

Reading Notes

caldron	a large kettle used for boiling
fetch	to go after something and bring it back

Vocabulary

1. The days were growing longer, but the cold was more **intense**. _____ extreme

2. In every maple tree Father had **bored** a small hole _____ drilled

3. gushing out their **aromatic** juice. _____ scented

4. the snow was **pitted** with water falling from the icicles _____ indented

5. "That's pretty good," Mother said, **beaming**. _____ smiling widely

Comprehension Questions

1. What does Almanzo love about being in the frozen wild woods? _____

   He loves trudging through the woods where no one has walked before and only his own tracks follow him. He also loves to collect and eat wintergreen berries.

2. Who comes to buy the potatoes? How many bushels are sold? For how much money? _____

   The New York potato-buyers arrive in Malone to buy locally grown potatoes. Father sells 500 bushels at a dollar a bushel, for a total of $500.

3. How do Almanzo and Alice make the work of loading the potatoes into baskets more fun? _____

   They raced against each other to see who can fill a basket the fastest.

4. List the Wilders' spring-cleaning chores. _____ They pull up carpets and clean them by beating them outdoors, move and clean everything in the house including curtains and bedding, clean the cellar, sort the vegetables in the cellar, scrub and whitewash the walls, and scour the butter tubs.

Quotations

"When the days begin to lengthen, the cold begins to strengthen."

At noon all the sap was boiling in the caldron. Father opened the lunch-pail, and Almanzo sat on the log beside him. They ate and talked. Their feet were stretched out to the fire, and a pile of logs was at their backs. All around them were snow and ice and wild woods, but they were snug and cosy.

Discussion Questions

1. Explain the first quote above.

2. Explain how maple syrup and maple sugar are made.

Enrichment

Focus Passage: Copy the second full paragraph on page 111 beginning with "At noon …" Spelling, punctuation, and capitalization should be perfect.

_____At noon all the sap was boiling in the caldron. Father opened the lunch-pail, and Almanzo sat on

the log beside him. They ate and talked. Their feet were stretched out to the fire, and a pile of logs was

at their backs. All around them were snow and ice and wild woods, but they were snug and cosy.

_____

_____

_____

_____

_____

_____

_____

_____

_____

Character: Character means <u>who</u> is in the story.

1. List the major characters in *Farmer Boy*. <u>Almanzo, Mother, Father, Royal, Eliza Jane, Alice</u>

2. List the minor characters in *Farmer Boy*. <u>Mr. Corse, Big Bill Ritchie, Pierre and Louis,</u>
   <u>Lazy John, French Joe</u>

Setting: Setting means the <u>time and place</u> in which the story happens.

1. Describe the general setting of *Farmer Boy*. _____
   <u>1860s, on a farm in New York state</u>

2. List the seasons that the Wilders have experienced thus far. _____
   <u>winter and very early spring</u>

Plot: Plot means <u>action</u> or <u>what happens</u> in the story.

Write out details about your favorite chapter in *Farmer Boy* so far. Use complete sentences.

_____

_____

_____

_____

_____

_____

_____

_____

_____

_____

_____

_____

_____

Drawing Page

Illustrate your favorite chapter from the previous page.

Vocabulary

Write the letter of the vocabulary word on the line in front of its definition.

1.	i	bragged	a.	contradict
2.	j	extreme	b.	charred
3.	d	destroyed	c.	racket
4.	m	scented	d.	demolished
5.	a	to speak against	e.	soberly
6.	w	quickly; with spirit	f.	drowsy
7.	p	walked with heavy feet	g.	pantry
8.	o	weight	h.	askew
9.	r	waking	i.	boasted
10.	y	small short-handled ax	j.	intense
11.	v	smooth; slick	k.	crevice
12.	f	sleepy	l.	quivering
13.	u	wrestling	m.	aromatic
14.	c	loud noise; clamor	n.	impudently
15.	s	moody	o.	heft
16.	g	area for food storage	p.	trudged
17.	e	seriously	q.	lavishly
18.	k	crack	r.	rousing
19.	x	calmly, peacefully	s.	sullen
20.	t	drilled	t.	bored
21.	b	partially burned	u.	scuffling
22.	h	bent to one side	v.	sleek
23.	l	trembling	w.	briskly
24.	q	generously; extravagantly	x.	placidly
25.	n	disrespectfully	y.	hatchet

Quiz 1 Review

Short Answer
Answer the following questions in complete sentences.

1. What is the setting of *Farmer Boy*? Where and in what year does it take place? _____

   The story is set in the year 1866. The story takes place in New York state.

   _____

   _____

2. Briefly describe the "surprise" that occurs at school involving Big Bill's gang and Mr. Corse. Big

   Bill and his gang threaten the teacher, but Mr. Corse surprises and defeats them with a bullwhip.

   _____

   _____

   _____

3. How do the Wilders keep the ice frozen even in the hot summer months? _____

   They stack the blocks of ice and pack them in sawdust in the ice-house.

   _____

   _____

   _____

4. What is Almanzo's "splendid" idea concerning his calves, and why does it go wrong? _____

   Almanzo decides to see if his team of calves can pull his sled with passengers on it because Star

   and Bright are behaving so well. He has forgotten to teach them to obey his commands while he

   is riding behind them. He finds this out after his sled crashes.

   _____

   _____

   _____

5. Why doesn't Father trust Almanzo around the colts? What does he fear will happen? ____ Father

   knows that young, unbroken horses are easily spoiled. If a careless boy scares or strikes a colt it

   could make it difficult or impossible to train well later.

   _____

   _____

Reading Notes

harrow	a farm machine with sharp teeth used to break up and level plowed ground; it is also used as a verb to describe the process of preparing the soil for planting
dinner-horn	a simple wind instrument used to call field workers home for a meal
seed corn	kernels of corn used for planting

Vocabulary

1. the sun was rising beyond the **dewy** meadows <u>wet with morning dew</u>

2. They dribbled the carrot seeds into the **furrows** <u>plowed rows</u>

3. All the soil must be made **mellow** and fine and smooth. <u>moist and rich in nutrients</u>

4. **Hustle** along there, son <u>hurry</u>

5. Almanzo … went up and down the long field, **straddling** the little furrows. <u>walking with one foot on either side</u>

Comprehension Questions

1. The experienced work horses know exactly what to do in the fields. Why would Almanzo have enjoyed driving them more if this weren't the case? <u>Almanzo enjoys the responsibility of training and directing the farm animals in their work. It makes him feel older and important. These mature horses don't need his direction; they can do their work without much guidance.</u>

2. Why do the farmers have to hurry to plant their good seeds? <u>Farmers have to get their good seeds started before the wild seeds (weeds, etc.) take over. Good seeds have to be nurtured, directed, and cared for. Bad seeds grow easily and can take off in any wild direction.</u>

3. What are the three fields of grain Father sows? What are they used for? <u>He sows a field of wheat for white bread, a field of rye for rye'n'injun bread, and a field of oats and peas to feed the livestock in winter.</u>

4. Explain the connection between ash leaves, squirrel ears, and corn planting. <u>Almanzo has learned that when the leaves of the ash tree are the size of a squirrel's ear, it's time to plant corn.</u>

Lesson 11: Springtime

Quotations

Almanzo was a little soldier in this great battle. From dawn to dark he worked, from dark to dawn he slept, then he was up again and working.

But Almanzo had never planted corn before. He did not handle the hoe so well. He had to trot two steps where Royal or Father took one … But he knew he would plant corn as fast as anybody, when his legs were longer.

Discussion Questions

1. The third paragraph of this chapter describes the work horses. Explain the phrase "wise, sober mares."

2. The first quote above describes Almanzo as a soldier in a battle. What is the battle, and in what way is he like a soldier in this battle?

3. Describe how the potatoes are planted.

Enrichment

Composition: Reread the last paragraph on page 128, beginning with "The seeds were too small …" In three to five sentences, retell the story of the lazy boy in your own words. Be sure to include the consequence of his actions.

_____

_____

_____

_____

_____

_____

_____

_____

_____

_____

_____

_____

Reading Notes

| colander | a bowl-shaped kitchen utensil with holes for draining off liquids |
| solder | to join metal objects using heated metal |

Vocabulary

1. the young horses … **whinnied** to the big white horse. _____ neighed _____

2. Nick Brown, the tin-**peddler**, was a jolly, fat man _____ traveling salesman _____

3. Mother was a good, **shrewd** trader. _____ crafty; clever _____

4. The big white horse stepped out **eagerly** _____ with anticipation _____

5. The red cart went past the house and **lurched** into the road _____ rolled or pitched suddenly; jerked _____

Comprehension Questions

1. Who is Nick Brown? Why are the Wilders eager to see him? _____ Nick Brown is the tin-peddler, and he always brings news from his travels, as well as entertaining stories and songs. In addition, he brings items the Wilders need.

2. Describe some of the wares the peddler brings. _____ On the peddler's wagon are pails, pans, basins, cups, dippers, skimmers, strainers, steamers, colanders, graters, horns, whistles, and toy animals—all kinds of goods made of tin.

3. Where does the peddler get the tin ware he sells? _____
   He makes them himself during each winter.

4. What does Mother use instead of money to trade with the peddler? _____
   She trades clean, soft rags from her rag-bag.

5. Describe the way Mother and Mr. Brown bargain. Who wins? _____
   They laugh, joke, talk, and have a good time. Mother asks for more than she wants in order to get him to bargain with her. She doesn't really want the dishpan; it is a bargaining tactic.

Quotations

"I'll tell story for story and sing song for song, as long as you'll bring men up against me, and when they're all done, I'll tell the last story and sing the last song."

Who said this?   <u>Nick Brown, the tin-peddler</u>

For a long time they talked and argued. … For every pile of rags that Nick Brown added to the big pile, Mother asked more tinware than he wanted to trade her. They were both having a good time, joking and laughing and trading.

Discussion Questions

1. Think back to the types of wares the peddler brings. Does your family use any of these items? Are there items he sells that we don't use at all anymore?

2. What would the life of a peddler be like? Would it be an adventure or a chore? Why?

3. What kinds of people might a peddler meet on his journeys?

Enrichment

Literary Terms:
Alliteration is the intentional repetition of a beginning consonant sound. An example is shown below:

Mr. Brown … rubbed him down with <u>cl</u>ean <u>cl</u>oths.

In the sentences below, underline the beginning consonant sounds that are repeated.

1. Almanzo and Royal put on their <u>c</u>oats and <u>c</u>aps and <u>m</u>ufflers and <u>m</u>ittens.

2. He <u>b</u>lubbered and <u>b</u>egged.

3. He was a big, rough man with a <u>l</u>oud voice and a <u>l</u>oud <u>l</u>augh.

4. <u>T</u>en stacks of pancakes rose in <u>t</u>all <u>t</u>owers.

5. Almanzo <u>w</u>alked <u>w</u>histling behind his team.

6. <u>A</u>lice and <u>A</u>lmanzo carried <u>p</u>ails full of <u>p</u>ieces of <u>p</u>otato.

7. There were <u>t</u>in horns, <u>t</u>in whistles, <u>t</u>oy <u>t</u>in dishes and <u>p</u>atty-<u>p</u>ans.

8. Every piece was good thick tin, well made and <u>s</u>olidly <u>s</u>oldered.

9. Mother was short and <u>p</u>lump and <u>p</u>retty.

10. The <u>c</u>old was <u>c</u>ruel.

Reading Notes

"full of ginger"	lively; energetic
sha'n't / 'twa'n't	slang contractions for "shall not" and "it was not"
Providence	a term referring to God

Vocabulary

1. Then there were the **mangers** and stalls to clean _____ open boxes holding feed for livestock

2. Something or somebody's **prowling** round this house! ___ sneaking

3. they all heard a **stealthy** sound _____ sly, secretive

4. she heard a low, **savage** growl. _____ fierce

5. I made **inquiry**, and he was at the hotel _____ question

Comprehension Questions

1. Describe the appearance of the horse-buyer. __The horse-buyer is dressed in city clothes and taps__ his tall boots with a little red whip. He has black, closely-set eyes, a thin nose, a pointy black beard and a mustache that is waxed and twisted at the ends.

2. What does his appearance lead you to predict about his personality? _____ He looks slick, sly, and untrustworthy.

3. Why is supper time not as cheerful as usual on the night the horses are sold? _____ The family (especially Mother) is worried about having the money they'd received from the sale of the horses in the house overnight instead of in the bank.

4. Describe the strange dog. How does he help the Wilder family? __It is a big, thin dog with ribs__ showing. He protects the family from potential thieves.

5. What does Father learn when he arrives in Malone? _____ Father learns that another farmer had been robbed after dealing with the horse trader.

Quotations

Almanzo knew that in the whole world there was nothing so beautiful, so fascinating, as beautiful horses. When he thought that it would be years and years before he could have a little colt to teach and take care of, he could hardly bear it.

"Broken to drive double or single. They're high-spirited, full of ginger, and gentle as kittens. A lady can drive them."

Who said this? ___Father___   About what? ___his horses___

Discussion Questions

1. *In what small way does Father acknowledge that Almanzo is becoming more trustworthy around the young horses?

2. How is Father's bargaining with the horse-buyer similar to Mother's trading for tin-ware?

3. Why do you think Mother hears the noise in the middle of the night, but Father sleeps soundly?

Enrichment

Focus Passage: Copy the third paragraph on page 142, beginning with "Almanzo knew that ..." Spelling, punctuation, and capitalization should be perfect.

Almanzo knew that in the whole world there was nothing so beautiful, so fascinating, as beautiful horses. When he thought it would be years and years before he could have a little colt to teach and take care of, he could hardly bear it.

Reading Notes

bleating	the crying of a sheep
fleece	the wool coat of a sheep
Merinos	a breed of sheep with long, fine wool

Vocabulary

1. It was time to **shear** sheep. _____ to cut wool from _____

2. they **boosted** it up the bank _____ pushed

3. they scattered up the **slope** _____ side of a small hill

4. He didn't mean to **idle** _____ to be inactive

5. Father spoke to him **sternly**. _____ firmly; severely

Comprehension Questions

1. Sheep washing is like an assembly line. What is each person's job? _____

   Almanzo pushes each sheep through a gate. The men soap and rinse each one in the river. Then the sheep are herded to the river bank where the men help them out of the water.

   _____

   _____

2. In what way are Father's sheep special? How does that make shearing them a greater challenge?

   They are prize Merinos with the finest wool. They are a challenge because their skin lies in deep wrinkles and is hard to shear without cutting the animal.

   _____

3. What causes Almanzo to fall behind in his work? _____ He is outnumbered by two very good shearers who work so fast that he can't keep up. He is also distracted by the cat and her new kittens.

4. What is the trick Almanzo plays on John? _____ He hides one sheep so Lazy John can't finish first. He has taken the fleece up to the loft (even though it is still on the sheep) but Lazy John hasn't sheared it yet.

Quotations

Washing sheep was fun for everybody but the sheep. The men splashed and shouted and laughed in the water, and the boys ran and shouted in the pasture. The sun was warm on their backs and the grass was cool under bare feet, and all their laughter was small in the wide, pleasant stillness of the green fields and meadows.

"He laughs best who laughs last!"

Who said this? <u>Father</u>   To whom? <u>Almanzo and Lazy John</u>

Discussion Questions

1. Why do the men wash the sheep in the river instead of in tubs? Why are they washed before shearing instead of afterwards?

2. Why do you think Father laughs and says Almanzo can't keep up with the others after he has just sternly told him to do so? Do his words have the desired effect?

3. Why does Father think Almanzo's joke on Lazy John is so funny?

4. Explain why sheep are so important to the Wilder family.

Enrichment

Composition: Sheep shearing is complex work. Describe the steps in their correct order. Write complete sentences, using words like **first, next, then,** and **finally**.

<u>Answers will vary.</u>

<u>First, they wash the sheep in the river.</u>

<u>Next, Father and Lazy John shear off the wool.</u>

<u>Then, Royal rolls the fleece tightly and ties it with twine.</u>

<u>Finally, Almanzo carries it upstairs and lays it on the loft floor.</u>

Reading Notes

card / **carding machine** the process and/or the implement used to brush, clean, and disentangle the short fibers of wool

lye a strong solution obtained from filtering water through wood ashes; used in soap-making

ewes female sheep

Vocabulary

1. Only small children went to the spring **term** of school _____grading period; semester_____

2. He watched the moon **anxiously** _____ with anxiety; with worry _____

3. No one had ever **taken such pains** with carrots as he did _to be very careful_

4. Two **acres** of corn Almanzo hoed_____ acre: an area of land; 4840 square yards

5. right up to their **frail** lavender blossoms. _____ fragile _____

Comprehension Questions

1. What are some of nature's signs that something is going wrong with springtime?_____

    Dawns are chilly; noonday sun is cold; trees unfold leaves slowly; garden vegetables will not

    grow; corn grows slowly; wild strawberry blossoms are killed by frost.

2. Why does Almanzo anxiously await the dark of the moon? In the dark of the moon in May, he

    can stay home from school and plant pumpkins.

3. What is Almanzo trying to avoid and how does he avoid it? Almanzo doesn't want to go

    back to school. He works very slowly and does as much farmwork as he can find to do.

4. How are Father's fears justified about the slow-growing corn?_____

    The hard freeze comes in the night and threatens to kill the entire corn crop.

5. How do the Wilders save most of the corn crop? Why do they lose the last quarter acre? _____

    They pour cold water on every hill of corn to save each small plant from frostbite. They run out of

    time when the sun comes up before the last section is finished.

Quotations

Father and Mother and Royal and Eliza Jane and Alice and Almanzo filled their pails with water, and they all went to work, as fast as they could.

What was this work? pouring water on the corn

Almanzo ran to fill his pail; he ran back. He ran down the rows, splashing water on the hills of corn. His shoulders ached and his arm ached and there was a pain in his side. The soft earth hung on to his feet. He was terribly hungry. But every splash of water saved a hill of corn.

Discussion Questions

1. Explain Mother's process for soap-making.

2. What is meant by the sentence "The sun was coming to kill the corn"?

3. Reread the two quotes above. Why do you think the Wilders are able to save most of the corn even though there are thousands of hills of it and they don't start working until the middle of the night? Why is it so important to them to save it?

Enrichment

Dictation: Listen carefully as your teacher reads aloud. As she reads, write down what you hear. Pay close attention to spelling, capitalization and punctuation. When finished, compare your paragraph to the book, and circle any errors.

"They rode sleepily down to the barns. Almanzo was not quite awake yet, and he was tired and cold

and hungry. His hands were clumsy, doing the chores. But most of the corn was saved."

(last paragraph, p. 172)

_____

_____

_____

_____

_____

_____

_____

Reading Notes

parasol	light-weight umbrella used for shielding from the sun
Congressman	a member of Congress; a political figure
Declaration of Independence	the document that announced the independence of the American colonies from the British Empire
Redcoat	a British soldier serving during the American Revolution
musket	type of gun
Revolution	refers to the American Revolution

Vocabulary

1. They passed gray … and **dappled**-gray horses. _____ spotted _____

2. Almanzo felt solemn and very **proud**. _____ deeply satisfied _____

3. The music was so **gay**… _____ happy _____

4. I'd just as **lief** ask him if I wanted to. _____ readily; willingly _____

5. He was **faint-hearted**, but he had to go. _____ cowardly _____

Comprehension Questions

1. Once they arrive in Malone, why does Almanzo stay with Father instead of hurrying off like the rest of the family? He helps Father unhitch the horses because he would rather help with the horses than do anything else.

2. How does Frank get Almanzo to ask for the nickel? _____
   Frank dares Almanzo to ask for it. In fact, he double-dares him.

3. Why does Father ask Almanzo about potatoes? What does this have to do with the half-dollar?
   Father wants to make sure Almanzo understands how much work goes into the earning of money.
   He wants him to think about its value and spend his money wisely.

4. How does Almanzo decide to spend his half-dollar? He decides to buy a little suckling pig.

Quotations

All the country had a holiday air. Nobody was working in the fields, and along the road the people in their Sunday clothes were driving to town.

"It was farmers that took all that country and made it America. … But we were farmers, son; we wanted the land. It was farmers that went over the mountains, and cleared the land, and settled it, and farmed it, and hung on to their farms."

Who said this? Father

Discussion Questions

1. Explain how Independence Day is celebrated in the town of Malone. What are the main events during the celebration?

2. How do Frank and Mr. Paddock respond similarly in this chapter?

3. Using the second quote above, explain Father's earlier statement: "It was axes and plows that made this country."

Enrichment

Literary Terms:
Onomatopoeia occurs when a word imitates a sound or sounds like what it describes. For example:

pop   hiss   crack   sizzle

In each sentence below, underline words that are examples of onomatopoeia.

1. The fifes tooted and the flutes shrilled.

2. The drummer beat rat-a-tat-tat and rub-a-dub-dub on the drum.

3. The Stars and Stripes fluttered and flapped.

4. Then came buglers blowing and fifers tootling.

5. Then — BOOM!

6. Grandmother told us to hush.

7. Several small logs in the fire crackled at once.

8. We saw bees buzz wildly around their heads.

9. The whole hive murmured.

10. Leaves rustled as the squirrel moved through them.

*Ask students if they can think of any other examples of onomatopoeia.

Reading Notes

laid by	set aside for future use
bridles / **harness**	gear fitted on a horse, used to guide it during farm labor
"tan your jacket"	to be disciplined with a switch; a severe spanking

Vocabulary

1. they carefully made a little **slit** on the underside of the vine. __small cut__

2. Then he put a candle **wick** in the milk __central cord that burns or draws fuel__

3. he wouldn't teach them to jump, or **balk** __to stop short and refuse to go on__

4. I did lay out to **cultivate** the carrots and mend fence. __to prepare; to tend__

5. Almanzo … watched the raindrops **dimpling** the water. __making indentations in__

Comprehension Questions

1. Why does Almanzo try to eat so much? __Almanzo tries to eat more food so that he can grow up__ __faster. He hopes that Father will then let him help break the colts.__

2. Who is Starlight? What does Father say when Almanzo tries to touch him? __Starlight is Beauty's__ __foal. Father tells Almanzo he'll be in trouble if he ever tries to touch him again. Father doesn't__ __want to have to break the colt of any bad habits.__

3. Why doesn't Almanzo ask his father about fishing? __He thinks Father will say it is wrong to waste__ __time in idleness such as fishing.__

4. What does Almanzo have to do on rainy days? Why? __He has to churn milk. The cows are__ __giving so much milk that churning needs to be done twice a week. Mother and the girls are tired__ __of churning, so Almanzo gives them a break on rainy days.__

Quotations

Nothing ever smelled so good as the rain on clover. Nothing ever felt so good as raindrops on Almanzo's face, and the wet grass swishing around his legs. Nothing ever sounded so pleasant as the drops pattering on the bushes along Trout River, and the rush of the water over the rocks.

To what does this refer?   Father and Almanzo's fishing trip

"All work and no play makes Jack a dull boy. Tomorrow we'll go berrying."

Who said this?   Father

Discussion Questions

1. *What does Father teach Almanzo about growing pumpkins? Explain the process.

2. Explain the second quote above.

3. Describe the family berrying excursion and Almanzo's surprise encounter.

Enrichment

Focus Passage: Copy the last four paragraphs in the chapter (page 202) beginning with "It's time Mother and I ..." Spelling, punctuation, and capitalization should be perfect.

"It's time Mother and I had a vacation. We're thinking of spending a week at Uncle Andrew's. Can you children take care of things and behave yourselves while we're gone?"

"I'm sure Eliza Jane and Royal can look after the place for a week," Mother said, "with Alice and Almanzo to help them."

Almanzo looked at Alice, and then they both looked at Eliza Jane. Then they all looked at Father and said:

"Yes, Father."

Reading Notes

rind   the tough outer skin of some fruits
yearling   an animal that is one year old
wabbling   means the same as "wobbling"; unsteady

Vocabulary

1. they **lugged** them one by one to the ice house _____ dragged burdensomely

2. The air shimmered and **wavered** with heat _____ flickered or glimmered

3. Even Alice was **horrified** because he had wasted candy _____ shocked

4. Goodness! don't **dawdle** so! _____ to waste time; to be slow

5. "I guess I was **aggravating**," she said. "But I didn't mean to be." _____ greatly annoying

Comprehension Questions

1. How do the children initially feel after their parents leave? What do they do first? They feel very alone and a little scared. The first thing they do is make ice cream.

2. Who is Lucy? What happens when Almanzo feeds her candy? _____ Lucy is Almanzo's pig. When he feeds her candy, it is so sticky that she can't open her mouth and therefore can't eat. She is frightened, so they have to chase her to catch her and pry the candy out of her mouth.

3. Why are the children in a frenzy on the last day before Mother and Father return? _____ They have created such a mess and have neglected their chores. They have to put the place in order before their parents arrive.

4. What happens between Almanzo and Eliza Jane in the parlor? _____ Almanzo reacts against Eliza Jane's "bossing" and throws the stove polish brush at her, leaving a black stain on the parlor wallpaper. He worries that she will tell on him when his parents see it, but she secretly patches the wallpaper to cover up for him.

Quotations

"Well, Mother told you to obey me. And I'm not going to waste melon rinds on any pig! I'm going to make watermelon-rind preserves."

Who said this? _____Eliza Jane_____   To whom? _____Almanzo_____

"I guess I was aggravating," she said. "But I didn't mean to be. You're the only little brother I've got."

Who said this? _____Eliza Jane_____   To whom? _____Almanzo_____

Discussion Questions

1. What does Almanzo do as soon as he thinks no one is watching him? What happens?

2. What do Alice and Almanzo do in the parlor? Why do they hide their activity from Eliza Jane?

3. How does Almanzo's guilty conscience punish him when the Webbs come to visit?

4. Based on the entire chapter and the quotes above, is Eliza Jane a good sister to Almanzo? Why or why not?

Enrichment

Literary Terms:
Similes are expressions that compare two different things using "like" or "as."

In each sentence, circle "like" or "as," and underline the things being compared.

1. The <u>dark</u> hung (like) a <u>mist</u> over the field.

2. Their white <u>blossoms</u> were (like) <u>foam</u> on the field.

3. Their nostrils fluttered when they breathed; their <u>ears</u> moved (as) swiftly as <u>birds.</u>

4. Clean sheep scattered up the slope, making the <u>pasture</u> look (like) a snowball <u>bush</u> in bloom.

5. Quick (as) <u>black lightning</u> the <u>lash</u> circled and struck and coiled again.

6. He oiled their curved <u>hoofs</u>, till they shone black (as) Mother's polished <u>stove.</u>

7. The <u>shocks</u> looked (like) little Indian <u>wigwams</u>.

8. <u>They're</u> high-spirited, full of ginger, and gentle (as) <u>kittens</u>.

9. Pork-pickle had a stinging <u>smell</u> that felt (like) a <u>sneeze</u>.

10. The little <u>pig</u> was as white (as) a <u>lamb</u>, and she liked Almanzo.

Reading Notes

scythe	a farm tool with a long, curved blade used for mowing or reaping
timothy	a type of grass, cultivated for use as hay
whetstone	a hard stone used to sharpen tools
bombazine	a dressy fabric made of silk and cotton

Vocabulary

1. the **plumed** timothy fell in great swathes. _____ feathery _____

2. and the plumed timothy fell in great **swathes**. _____ sections, rows _____

3. Now the men **whetted** their scythes _____ sharpened _____

4. Everything must be saved, nothing wasted of all the summer's **bounty**. generous amount

5. Father and Royal could bind oats as fast as the **reapers** cut them. ____ crop harvesters ____

Comprehension Questions

1. Explain what Mother's dinner horn means when it blows in mid-morning. _____

   Mother blows her dinner horn in mid-morning to let the workers know the egg-nog is ready. _____

   _____

2. When the heavy pail of egg-nog threatens to spill, how does Almanzo solve the problem? What is

   his reasoning? He solves his problem by drinking some of the egg-nog so the pail won't be so full.

   He reasons that spilling it would be wasteful, and Mother says waste is sinful.

   _____

3. Give reasons why Almanzo likes summer haying-time. _____

   Almanzo loves the variety of the work and the long days.   He loves the egg-nog too. _____

   _____

4. What is the difference between sheaves and shocks? Why do the oats have to be shocked before

   dark?   Sheaves are tied bundles of grain, while shocks are stacks of sheaves formed for the

   purpose of drying the grain. The oats would ruin if they lay in the dew on the ground overnight.

   _____

   _____

Quotations

There was no rest and no play for anyone now. They all worked from candle-light to candle-light. … Everything must be saved, nothing wasted of all the summer's bounty.

Mother did not do any bargaining at all. She said, proudly: "My butter speaks for itself."

Discussion Questions

1. Explain Lazy John's words when he says, "That puts heart into a man!"

2. Name all the work that must be done during the early harvest time.

3. Describe the butter-buyer's visit. Why does Mother make a trip to town afterwards? Why is this unusual?

Enrichment

Poetry Connection: "The Hayloft" by Robert Louis Stevenson is a delightful poem of a child at play in a hayloft. Almanzo may have spent time in this same way.

Do the following:

1. Find the poem "The Hayloft" in the Appendix.

2. Read it through several times.

3. Discuss the meanings of the words, the aspects of poetry, and its message.

4. Copy it carefully and precisely.

5. Then memorize it, so that you may enjoy it in the future, whenever you wish.

Reading Notes

harvest moon	the full moon that occurs nearest the autumnal equinox
hogshead	a large barrel or cask with a capacity ranging from 63-140 gallons
poultice	a soft, moist pack of medicinal herbs, applied to a wound to aid in healing

Vocabulary

1. Alice put on her hood and **shawl**. _____ cloth worn as a head and shoulder covering

2. cold wind blew **gritty** dust into Almanzo's eyes. _____ sandy

3. Alice held out her **grubby** hands to warm them_____ dirty

4. It stuck on his face, **scalding hot.** _____ hot enough to burn

5. "I guess it's your potato," he **snuffled**. _____ breathed noisily; sniffed

Comprehension Questions

1. Explain why the perfect apples are picked, hauled, and stored very carefully. How are the
   imperfect apples used? _____ If an apple is bruised, it will rot, and the rot will spread to all of the
   apples; so one bad apple could spoil the entire crop. The imperfect apples are used to make cider.

2. Why is Father in a hurry to harvest potatoes? _____ There is a threat of frost, and a frost will kill the
   potatoes, forcing Mr. Wilder to purchase potatoes.

3. How can Almanzo usually tell the time of day while outdoors? Why doesn't this method work when
   they are digging potatoes? _____ He looks at the placement of the sun in the sky. It doesn't work
   because it is a cloudy day.

4. How does Almanzo get blistered? Almanzo gets blistered when a roasting potato bursts and hits
   his eye.

5. Why does Almanzo insist on sharing the remaining potato with Alice?_____
   He feels guilty because he had been acting selfishly and standing by the warm fire while Alice was
   working alone.

Quotations

"No, it's yours. It was my potato that exploded." ... "This one's yours because you're hurt, and I'm not hungry, anyway not very hungry."

Who said this? ___Alice___   To whom? ___Almanzo___

All the harvest was in, now. Cellar and attic and the barns were stuffed to bursting. Plenty of food, and plenty of feed for all the stock, was stored away for the winter.

Discussion Questions

1. Which crops are stored in the cellar? in the barn? in the attic? How is each type of food used?

2. What does Mother mean when she says, "A miss is as good as a mile"?

Enrichment

Quotation Review: How good is your memory?

For each of the following quotations, write the name of the person who said it. Look up the answer in the book if you need help.

1. "I'll tell story for story and sing song for song ..." ___Nick Brown___ (Ch. 12)

2. "All right, two hundred it is. I'll lose money by it, but here you are." ___horse buyer___ (Ch. 13)

3. "It's work, son. That's what money is; it's hard work." ___Father___ (Ch. 16)

4. "I guess I know how to handle my own calves." ___Almanzo___ (Ch. 9)

5. "This one's yours because you're hurt ..." ___Alice___ (Ch. 20)

6. "When a man undertakes a job, he has to stick to it till he finishes it." ___Father___ (Ch. 4)

7. "I dare you to ask him." ___Frank___ (Ch. 16)

8. "You mean to say we must keep all that money in the house overnight!" ___Mother___ (Ch. 13)

9. "Stay in at recess and learn it." ___Mr. Corse___ (Ch. 1)

10. "They're high-spirited, full of ginger, and gentle as kittens." ___Father___ (Ch. 13)

11. "I guess I was aggravating. But I didn't mean it." ___Eliza Jane___ (Ch. 18)

12. "There's the fleece! I've got it upstairs and you haven't sheared it! I beat you! I beat you!"

   ___Almanzo___ (Ch. 14)

Elements of Literature

Character: Character means <u>who</u> is in the story.

Identify the characters new to *Farmer Boy* since Lesson 10.

<u>horse-buyer</u>   <u>strange dog</u>

<u>tin-peddler (Nick Brown)</u>   <u>cousin Frank</u>

<u>Mr. Paddock</u>

Setting: Setting means the <u>time</u> and <u>place</u> in which the story happens.

1. Describe the Wilders' farm at the turn of the year. <u>The days are getting longer, there is more intense cold, sap begins to rise in the trees, and the snow softens and begins melting.</u>

2. Describe the Wilders' farm in the spring. <u>The meadows are dewy, the fields are lumpy and need harrowing, the weather is warmer, and the leaves begin budding.</u>

3. Describe the Wilders' farm in the summer. <u>The sunshine is hot, plants are growing quickly, and the berries are ready to be picked.</u>

4. Describe the Wilders' farm in the fall. <u>The crops are ripe, there is a frosty chill in the air, and the plants in the garden are ripe.</u>

Plot: Plot means <u>action</u> or <u>what happens</u> in the story.

Write about your favorite story in Chapters 11-20 of *Farmer Boy*. Use complete sentences.

_____

_____

_____

_____

_____

_____

_____

_____

_____

Drawing Page

Illustrate each season in the space provided below.

Turn of the Year

Spring

Summer

Fall

Vocabulary

Write the letter of the vocabulary word on the line in front of its definition.

1.	__h__	sandy	a.	cultivate
2.	__c__	plowed rows	b.	frail
3.	__s__	flickered or glimmered	c.	furrows
4.	__n__	roll or pitch suddenly; jerked	d.	swathes
5.	__d__	sections, rows	e.	shrewd
6.	__i__	cowardly	f.	balk
7.	__e__	crafty; clever	g.	sternly
8.	__f__	to stop short and refuse to go on	h.	gritty
9.	__y__	hot enough to burn	i.	faint-hearted
10.	__p__	sly; secretive	j.	hustle
11.	__o__	generous amount	k.	whetted
12.	__v__	grading period; semester	l.	shear
13.	__m__	to waste time; to be slow	m.	dawdle
14.	__r__	walking with one foot on either side	n.	lurched
15.	__u__	greatly annoying	o.	bounty
16.	__k__	sharpened	p.	stealthy
17.	__l__	cut wool from	q.	slit
18.	__j__	hurry	r.	straddling
19.	__a__	to prepare; to tend	s.	wavered
20.	__b__	fragile	t.	inquiry
21.	__g__	firmly; severely	u.	aggravating
22.	__w__	spotted	v.	term
23.	__q__	small cut	w.	dappled
24.	__x__	traveling salesman	x.	peddler
25.	__t__	question	y.	scalding-hot

Short Answer
Answer the following questions in complete sentences.

1. In what small way does Father acknowledge that Almanzo is becoming more trustworthy around the young horses? Father allows him to help groom the four-year-old colts to get them ready for the horse-buyer.

2. Sheep shearing is done as an assembly line. What is each person's job? Almanzo pushes each sheep through a gate. The men soap and rinse each one in the river. Then the sheep are herded to the river bank where the men help them out of the water.

3. Briefly describe what Father teaches Almanzo about growing pumpkins. He cuts a slit in the pumpkin vine and sticks a candle wick into it. The other end of the wick is placed in a pan of milk. The milk is wicked up into the vine and consumed by the growing pumpkin, causing it to grow faster and larger than it would have simply by consuming liquid from the vine through the natural process.

4. What happens between Almanzo and Eliza Jane in the parlor? Almanzo reacts against Eliza Jane's "bossing" and throws the stove polish brush at her, leaving a black stain on the parlor wallpaper. He worries that she will tell on him when his parents see it, but she secretly patches the wallpaper to cover up for him.

5. Explain why the perfect apples are picked, hauled, and stored very carefully. How are the imperfect apples used? If an apple is bruised, it will rot, and the rot will spread to all of the apples; so one bad apple could spoil the entire crop. The imperfect apples are used to make cider.

Reading Notes

thoroughbred	a horse bred chiefly for racing
haunch	the back, upper leg and thigh of an animal
sulky	an open two-wheeled vehicle drawn by one horse, used in harness racing

Vocabulary

1. people were **clustered** like flies. _____ grouped ___

2. The ground there was **trodden** into deep dust by the crowd _____ trampled; worn down ___

3. Those long ears stood up above their long, **gaunt** faces_____ lean _____

4. Father **pried** off the cover of one barrel_____ opened with leverage ___

5. But I would rather get something more **substantial** for mine._____ valuable, lasting _____

Comprehension Questions

1. What is the first thing Almanzo wants to see at the fair?_____

   Almanzo first wants to see the horses._____

2. What makes Almanzo feel important and grown-up? _____

   He feels important talking about horses with Father._____

3. Describe the two black creatures Almanzo sees in the stall. What is a mule?_____

   They have bare tails, bristly manes, rabbit ears, long yellow teeth, and a squawking roar. A mule

   is a cross-breed—half horse, half donkey._____

4. Why does Almanzo feel "cold and small and scared" after winning? What does he soon realize?

   Almanzo is afraid he has won unfairly by feeding his pumpkin milk. He feels guilty, but he soon

   realizes that Father knew all about the milk, and Father wouldn't cheat._____

   _____

   _____

5. Why doesn't Almanzo enjoy the third day of the fair?_____ He is tired of having a good time,

   being dressed up, and leaving the farm. He is unsettled and wants to return to his normal routine.

   _____

   _____

Quotations

"What's the good of a horse that can pull a barn? We don't want to pull a barn. A Morgan has muscle enough to pull a wagon, and he's fast enough to pull a buggy, too." … Almanzo felt important and grown-up, talking horses with Father.

Who said this? Almanzo   About what?   the Belgian horses

Then he knew he was telling a lie. Father was hearing him tell a lie. He looked up at Mr. Paddock and said: "I raised it on milk. It's a milk-fed pumpkin. Is—is that all right?"

Who said this? Almanzo

Discussion Questions

1. *Why does the county fair take place after all the crops are harvested?

2. Explain what Father means when he says: "Never bet your money on another man's game."

3. Describe the horse race. Why doesn't Father believe in betting on a winner?

Enrichment

Focus Passage: Copy the sixth paragraph on page 271 ("Father's hand clapped …"). Spelling, punctuation, and capitalization should be perfect. Copy the quotation marks carefully as well.

Father's hand clapped on Almanzo's shoulder. All at once Almanzo could breathe, and he was tingling all over. Mr. Paddock was shaking his hand. All the judges were smiling. Ever so many people said, "Well, well, Mr. Wilder, so your boy's got first prize!"

Reading Notes

twilight   the diffused light in the sky during early morning or evening when the sun is below the horizon

Indian summer   a period of mild weather occurring in late autumn

Vocabulary

1. Alice put on her **cloak** and hood   cape

2. **delicate** bare limbs of the beeches.   fragile

3. Then he and Alice **trampled** down leaves again   stomped

4. **heaved** it out and laid it on boards.   lifted with difficulty

5. [The tubes] … **tapered** to a point at the bottom   pointed

Comprehension Questions

1. Why does bitter cold mean it is butchering-time?   The meat will freeze and stay frozen all winter.

2. What are some of the tasks Father does around the farm to prepare for winter?   He tightens the barn's windows, nails down loose boards, banks the walls of the barn and house with straw for insulation, and fits storm doors and windows on the house.

3. What does Father do with the beef hide?   He saves it to have shoes made from it later.

4. How are Lazy John and French Joe paid for their labor?   They are given some of the fresh meat to take home for their families.

5. What is the connection between pork fat, beef fat, tallow, and lard?   Pork fat is melted to make lard, which is used in cooking. Beef fat is melted for tallow to use in making candles.

Quotations

Before they had finished, Lazy John and French Joe had come, and there was time to snatch only a bite of breakfast. Five hogs and a yearling beef were to be killed that day.

All this time he was grinding sausagemeat. He poked thousands of pieces of meat into the grinder and turned the handle round and round, for hours and hours. He was glad when that was finished.

To whom does this refer? <u>Almanzo</u>

Discussion Questions

1. What is "poor man's fertilizer"? Why is snow plowed into unfrozen ground valuable?

2. How are the Wilders like the squirrels that are busy storing nuts for the winter?

3. Explain how butchering is done.

4. What is headcheese? What is mincemeat? Use the book to find your answers.

Enrichment

Interpreting a Passage: The Wilders make candles in a way that is unfamiliar to most people today. Learning about ways that are unfamiliar to us always increases our knowledge.

Read the paragraphs about candle-making, beginning from the top of page 283 to the end of the chapter. Then, list the seven steps of candle-making that the book describes.

1. Scrub the lard kettles and fill them with beef fat.

2. Prepare the candle-wicking for each tube.

3. Fasten the end of each wick tightly with a raw potato.

4. Pour in the hot tallow, filling each tube.

5. Set the molds outside to cool.

6. Dip the molds in boiling water and pull the formed candles out of the molds.

7. Cut the candles off the sticks and trim each wick separately.

Reading Notes

cobbler	one who mends or makes boots or shoes
indigo	a blue dye obtained from plants
carpet-bag	a traveling bag made of carpet fabric
tanned hides	chemically treated animal skins converted into leather

Vocabulary

1. Mother's **shears** went snickety-snick through the … cloth she had woven. ___scissors___

2. Almanzo helped Father **husk** corn. _____ remove outer leaves

3. She told Almanzo all about her lessons in music and **deportment** _____ manners

4. she was **mortified** because Father drank tea from his saucer. _____ embarrassed

5. if you **drudge** all your days on a farm _____ to do dull, tedious work

Comprehension Questions

1. Describe the cobbler. Why is he three weeks late? Why is Mother upset? _____ He is fat, good-natured, and tells jokes. He had been kept three weeks at one house making shoes for a wedding. Mother is upset because the children had to go to school without good shoes.

2. The Wilders make almost everything they use, so why don't they make their own shoes?_____ Cobbler's work is highly skilled and requires special equipment.

3. Where is the Academy located? Why don't the children live at home while attending? _____ The Academy is in Malone, five miles away. That distance is too far for them to travel on a daily basis.

4. What historic basis does Mother use for rebuking Eliza Jane's rude remark? _____ She explains that Dutch sailors brought saucers from China 200 years before and that people have been drinking from saucers ever since.

5. Why does Royal want to be a storekeeper and not a farmer?_____ He wants to dress nicely, stay clean, and be driven around town in a carriage.

Quotations

Dinner-time was gay. The cobbler told all the news, he praised Mother's cooking, and he told jokes till Father roared and Mother wiped her eyes. Then the cobbler asked Father what he should make first, and Father answered: "I guess you better begin with boots for Almanzo."

"It isn't the style to drink out of saucers any more," Eliza Jane said. "Nice people drink out of the cup."

Discussion Questions

1. *What is the significance of Father's announcement that Almanzo's boots should be made first?

2. This chapter describes some of the common tools used and the process of shoe making. Using the context of the story, try to answer the following questions: What is a *last*? What is a *vise*, and how is it used? What is an *awl*? What is a *rasp*? What does it mean to "bore a hole"?

Enrichment

Focus Passage – Dialogue:

When characters in a story talk to one another, it's called "dialogue." When writing dialogue, every time a new character speaks, a new paragraph is begun.

Carefully copy the dialogue between Mother and Eliza Jane on page 296, beginning with "It isn't the style …" and ending with "… where saucers come from." Watch indentations and punctuation!

"It isn't the style to drink out of saucers any more," Eliza Jane said. "Nice people drink out of the cup."

"Eliza Jane!" Alice cried. "Be ashamed! I guess Father's as nice as anybody!"

Mother actually stopped working. She took her hands out of the dishpan and turned round to face Eliza Jane.

"Young lady," she said, "if you have to show off your fine education, you tell me where saucers come from."

Reading Notes

timber	trees or wooded land considered as a source of wood
bobsled	a long sled made of two shorter sleds joined together, one behind the other
tongue	the harnessing pole attached to the front end of an animal-drawn vehicle

Vocabulary

1. First Father **hewed** the bottoms of the runners flat and smooth… chopped; carved

2. …clear around the **crook** of their turned-up front ends. curve or bend

3. Into the holes he drove **stout** wooden pegs. strong, sturdy

4. For the tongue he used an elm **sapling**,… a young tree

5. …elm is tougher and more **pliable** than oak. flexible

Comprehension Questions

1. Why does Almanzo want his very own bobsled?

   He wants to begin using his team of calves to help bring timber out of the woods.

2. Why does Father show Almanzo how to make the sled rather than make it for him?

   Father knows it is important for Almanzo to learn the skill. He also knows Almanzo will

   appreciate it more and take better care of it, as well as feel good about his accomplishment.

3. Why does Father use an elm sapling for the tongue?

   Elm is stonger and more flexible than oak, so it will hold up under the stress better.

4. Why does Almanzo want deep snow while it is storming?

   If the snow is deep, he can begin using his new bobsled.

Quotations

Snow was falling next morning when Almanzo rode with Father to the timber lot. Large feathery flakes made a veil over everything, and if you were alone and held your breath and listened, you could hear the soft, tiny sound of their falling.

The storm was rising. The falling snow whirled and the wind was crying with a lonely sound when Almanzo and Father carried the full milk-pails to the house that night.

Discussion Questions

1. Read the quotations above. What imagery does the author use to describe the snow? What is seen? What is heard? What is felt? To what are the snowflakes and the wind compared?

2. What specific kinds of trees are needed to build the bobsled?

3. Describe the little bobsled, using as many details as you can.

Enrichment

Dictation: Listen carefully as your teacher reads aloud. As she reads, write down what you hear. Pay close attention to indentation, spelling, capitalization and punctuation. When finished, compare your paragraph to the book and circle any errors.

In the whole timber lot there were no two trees alike.

"You wouldn't find two alike in the whole world, son," Father said. "Not even two blades of grass are the same. Everything is different from everything else, if you look at it."

Reading Notes

cud	food regurgitated from the stomach to the mouth and chewed again
flail	a manual threshing tool made up of a wooden handle with a shorter, free-swinging stick attached to its end
fanning-mill	a machine used to blow and separate chaff from the grain
hopper	a funnel-shaped container through which grain passes to a machine

Vocabulary

1. When Almanzo **latched** the door behind him… _secured; hooked_

2. The cows stood in a row, placidly swinging their **tasseled** tails _bound at one end with loose threads_

3. Father … **riveted** the ends together to make a leather loop. _fastened_

4. That's a lazy man's way to **thresh**. _to separate grain from chaff_

5. a cloud of **chaff** blew out its front _hard outer covering of grain_

Comprehension Questions

1. How do the barns stand undisturbed against the howling storm? _They have been built strong and solid to keep weather out and warmth inside._

2. According to Father, what is a lazy man's way to thresh grain? What is wrong with saving time?
   A threshing machine does the work more quickly, but Father believes that saving time would only mean being bored with nothing to do all winter.

3. What different crops are threshed and/or put through the fanning-mill? _They thresh wheat, oats, beans, and Canada peas. They also put beechnuts through the fanning-mill._

4. Describe how Almanzo feels while he spends time in the snug barns threshing and doing his chores. _He feels good knowing that he has helped to plant, harvest, and flail the grain. He also feels good knowing that he can take care of all the animals._

Quotations

"All it saves is time, son. And what good is time, with nothing to do?"

Who said this? ___Father___   About what? ___the new threshing machines___

Almanzo had harrowed the fields, he had helped in the harvest, and now he was threshing. He helped to feed the patient cows, and the horses eagerly whinnying over the bars of their stalls, and the hungrily bleating sheep, and the grunting pigs. And he felt like saying to them all: "You can depend on me. I'm big enough to take care of you all."

Discussion Questions

1. Describe how Father and Almanzo thresh grain. How is the flail used?

2. What is Almanzo likely to become when he grows up? What evidence supports your idea?

3. Is there a place that feels completely comfortable and familiar to you? Why?

Enrichment

Expressions to Know: Briefly explain what each of the following phrases means.

1. haste makes waste ___When you hurry at a task you often make careless mistakes that later have to be corrected. This wastes time rather than saving time.___

2. What good is time with nothing to do? ___Father thinks you should spend your time doing something beneficial rather than wasting time doing nothing and risk being bored.___

3. sit and twiddle your thumbs ___This is sitting with your hands folded and moving your thumbs around each other in a circular motion. It is an expression for wasting time.___

4. peck-measure ___a measurement; a peck is a unit of dry volume equal to 8 quarts___

5. You can depend on me. ___This means "I am reliable. You can be sure that I will do whatever it is that needs to be done."___

Reading Notes

horehound   a type of candy, made from a plant in the mint family

cravat   a band of fabric worn around the neck as a tie

dast   a slang term for "dare"

Vocabulary

1. Bad boys found nothing but **switches** in their stockings… ___sticks; small branches___

2. he could hardly stand the **strain**. _____ stress; pressure

3. He had to **scour** the steel knives and forks… _____ to polish by scrubbing

4. Almanzo's insides **quaked**. _____ shook violently

5. Spoons … **gouged** deep into the mashed potatoes…_____ roughly grooved or cut

Comprehension Questions

1. What does the threat of a switch have to do with Almanzo's good behavior? ____Switches or a____ trip to the woodshed means the same thing: a spanking. Almanzo behaves well to avoid this.

2. Why did Almanzo quake when he heard Mother's comment that he might spill the stove blacking? It reminds him of the time he made a mess of the parlor wall by throwing the stove polish brush.

3. Describe Christmas morning. Why does Father say to look at the clock? _____The children____ get up when Almanzo yells "Merry Christmas" and dashes downstairs. They empty their stockings and find presents there. They are very excited, and they wake Father and Mother up at 3:30 a.m.!

4. What does Frank dare Almanzo to do? What happens? _____Frank dares Almanzo to climb____ in and sit on Starlight's back. Almanzo knows better and refuses. Frank begins climbing on the stall, scaring Starlight. Almanzo pulls him down and they fight. Royal comes in and breaks up the fight.

Quotations

For a long time it seemed that Christmas would never come. On Christmas, Uncle Andrew and Aunt Delia, Uncle Wesley and Aunt Lindy, and all the cousins were coming to dinner. It would be the best dinner of the whole year. And a good boy might get something in his stocking.

"I guess I'd do it if I wanted to, if I was you. I guess your father wouldn't know."

Who said this? __Frank__   About what? __climbing on Starlight's back__

Discussion Questions

1. What gifts does Almanzo receive? Why are these "practical" gifts so important to him?

2. Why is anticipation sometimes both wonderful and difficult at the same time?

3. Name some of the foods Mother serves at Christmas dinner. Why does Almanzo think the adults are heartless?

4. Christmas traditions can vary from family to family as well as from culture to culture. Compare and contrast the Wilders' Christmas traditions with those of your own family.

Enrichment

Focus Passage: Copy the last full paragraph on page 315 ("But Almanzo was already ..."). Spelling, punctuation, and capitalization should be perfect.

But Almanzo was already running downstairs. Alice and Eliza Jane were flying from their room, but Almanzo beat them. He saw his sock hanging all lumpy; he set down the candle and grabbed his sock. The first thing he pulled out was a cap, a boughten cap!

Reading Notes

skid	timber used as a support or track for rolling heavy objects
cant-poles	long, sharp poles with a free-swinging iron hook at one end
topsy-turvy, pell-mell	both expressions mean a state of utter disorder; confusion
corded	cut to the same length and stacked

Vocabulary

1. he fed them carrots and talked to them **soothingly**. _in a calming manner_

2. You **spoil** a team if you let them see-saw. _ruin_

3. They snorted and **floundered** and plunged _struggled helplessly_

4. They snorted and floundered and **plunged** _fell forcefully_

5. But can you **figure**? _to calculate with numbers_

Comprehension Questions

1. Father's French neighbors come to help with the wood hauling. What other things (in previous chapters) have they helped the Wilders do? _They helped with ice cutting, butchering, and sheep shearing._

2. What is Almanzo's accident? How does his father react? _A log falls on him, hitting his head and crushing him into the snow. His father asks if he is hurt and then says that Almanzo should take more care next time._

3. What is Almanzo's reaction to his mother's suggestion that he stop work after his accident? _He is determined not to let a little accident stop him. But he works more slowly._

4. Almanzo has been taught to be patient and gentle with his oxen. What is an example of how his patience helps when things go wrong? _When his team begins to see-saw, he takes Joe's advice and speaks to them gently to settle them and get them to pull together. He speaks encouragingly to them when they make mistakes._

5. What is Almanzo's chief motivation for studying hard at arithmetic? _He knows that the sooner he learns it, the sooner he will be done with school._

Quotations

"Accidents will happen, son. Take more care next time. Men must look out for themselves in the timber."

Who said this? <u>Father</u>   To whom? <u>Almanzo</u>

He had to sit down and rest a minute. But he got up, and he petted Star and Bright and spoke to them encouragingly. He took an apple away from Pierre and broke it in two and gave it to the little steers. When they had eaten it, he cracked his whip and cheerfully shouted: "Giddap!"

To whom does this refer? <u>Almanzo</u>

Discussion Questions

1. Explain how logs are lifted onto the bobsleds to be hauled back to the farm.

2. What does Father do the first time he notices Almanzo struggling with his oxen in the ditch? What does he do the second time it happens? Why?

Enrichment

Sequencing: It is important, and often necessary, to remember the order of events in a story. Put the following events in order by numbering them from 1 to 8.

<u>5</u>   "Well, well, no bones broken!" Father said cheerfully.

<u>2</u>   Driving his own sled and oxen, Almanzo followed his father into the woods.

<u>4</u>   A log fell on Almanzo and smashed him into the snow.

<u>7</u>   Almanzo stayed patient with his team regardless of their mistakes.

<u>1</u>   Almanzo did not have to go to school because it was time to haul wood.

<u>8</u>   Once hauling was finished, Almanzo returned to school.

<u>3</u>   Almanzo searched for three straight poles to use for skids.

<u>6</u>   Star and Bright could not move because the sled was too heavily loaded.

Reading Notes

pocketbook	a pocket-sized case used to hold money and papers; a billfold
banknote	a note, promising to pay a sum on demand; accepted as money
liveryman	someone who works in a stable that boards horses

Vocabulary

1. You measly **skinflint**! _____ a person who is selfish with their money

2. Almanzo was so excited he **stammered**. _____ stuttered

3. The bills were **clutched** tight in his hand. _____ held tightly

4. And I figure the boy's **entitled** to it. _____ has a right to

5. And I'm much **obliged** to you, Paddock _____ thankful

Comprehension Questions

1. Why does Father sell some of his hay? Briefly explain how it is baled. ___Father has so much___ hay that his stock can't eat it all. The loose hay is put into a wooden box with levers. This machine squeezes the hay into bales. The bales are then tied together with ash-withes. _____

2. To what is Father referring when he tells Almanzo, "Learning is best put into practice"?_____ Father wants to give Almanzo the opportunity to go into town and actually sell the hay, based on his knowledge and mathematic skills. _____

3. What three questions does Father ask himself about the owner of the pocketbook? Who is the owner?_____ He asks himself who is suspicious of banks, who is tight with his money, and who has sold something valuable recently? Father guesses Mr. Thompson was the owner.

4. How does Almanzo bargain with the liveryman? _____ Almanzo uses the same bargaining trick he has seen Mother use with the tin-peddler. He asks for more money than he is willing to accept.

5. Why does Father initially object to Almanzo taking the money? _____ He says a person doesn't necessarily deserve a reward for common honesty.

Quotations

"Learning is best put into practice. What say you ride to town with me tomorrow, and sell that load of hay?"

Who said this? __Father__   To whom? __Almanzo__

Then he breathed a long sigh of relief, and said, "Well, this durn boy didn't steal any of it."

Who said this? __Mr. Thompson__   About whom? __Almanzo__

Discussion Questions

1. What does Father mean when he says, "Many a good beginning makes a bad ending"?

2. Mr. Case says, "I'd rather have a nimble sixpence than a slow shilling." What are sixpence and shillings? Explain the statement.

3. *What does Almanzo mean when he gives the nickel back and says, "I can't change it."? Why is he so angry at Mr. Thompson?

4. Reread the last two paragraphs of the chapter. What is Almanzo already planning to do with his money? Why is this exciting for the reader? How does the last line increase your desire to read on to the next chapter?

Enrichment

Learn More: Using the context of the story, study to find the definition of each of the words below. Then match the term to its correct definition.

1. __f__ a rotating spindle or shaft   a. hewed

2. __b__ a heavy, long-handled hammer used to pound stakes   b. maul

3. __c__ a flexible twig used to bind things together   c. withe

4. __h__ curved pieces of a harness around the neck of a draft animal   d. hay-baler

5. __d__ a person or machine that forms hay into bales   e. railroad press

6. __g__ a long pole attached to a pivot   f. capstan

7. __a__ cut or shaped with an ax   g. sweep

8. __e__ a box-shaped machine used for baling hay   h. hames

Reading Notes

wheelwright	one who builds and repairs wheels
"a piece of your mind"	an opinion; usually said with strong feeling or emotion
"at the beck and call of every Tom, Dick, and Harry"	always available at others' request and convenience

Vocabulary

1. It's a good **opening** for a smart young fellow. _____ opportunity _____

2. **Apprentice** him to me, and I'll treat the boy right._____ one who works in return for instruction _____

3. curled away from the **keen** edges of the planes. _____ sharp _____

4. How does Mr. Paddock make his money, if it isn't **catering** to us? ___ serving ____

5. **Truckling** to other people for his living _____ submitting; yielding _____

Comprehension Questions

1. What does Mr. Paddock discuss with Father? What does Almanzo like about Mr. Paddock's work?

   Mr. Paddock wants Almanzo to work for him as an apprentice. Almanzo thinks it is a cheerful

   place, he wouldn't have to go to school, and he would enjoy painting the wheels on buggies.

   _____

2. Why does Mother think moving to town is a step down from being a farmer?_____

   Town workers depend on others for their livelihood, while a farmer relies only on himself and the

   weather.

3. What does Almanzo dislike about the life of Mr. Paddock? _____

   Almanzo dislikes that Mr. Paddock has to please mean customers like Mr. Thompson.

4. What does Almanzo want more than anything in the world? How does he decide this? _____

   He wants to be like Father, free and independent. He knows he doesn't want to live inside walls

   and please people he doesn't like. He wants to own horses, cows, and fields.

   _____

5. What is Almanzo's request that convinces Father of his desire to be a farmer? _____

   He asks for a colt of his own to raise and train.

Quotations

"You ever think of making a wheelwright out of him?"

Who said this? ___Mr. Paddock___   About whom? ___Almanzo___

"A farmer depends on himself, and the land and the weather. If you're a farmer, you raise what you eat, you raise what you wear, and you keep warm with wood out of your own timber. You work hard, but you work as you please, and no man can tell you to go or come. You'll be free and independent, son, on a farm."

Who said this? ___Father___   To whom? ___Almanzo___

Discussion Questions

1. *Compare and contrast Mother's and Father's hopes for Almanzo's future.

2. *Father is fair and honest with Almanzo about his options. How does he explain city life? How does he explain farm life?

3. After reading *Farmer Boy*, what do you find appealing about farm life?

Enrichment

Poetry Connection: "The Happy Farmer" summarizes the joys of farming in a beautifully poetic way.

Do the following:

1. Find the poem "The Happy Farmer" in the Appendix.

2. Read it through several times.

3. Discuss the meanings of the words, the aspects of poetry, and its message.

4. Copy it carefully and precisely.

5. Then memorize it, so that you may enjoy it in the future, whenever you wish.

Elements of Literature

Character: Character means <u>who</u> is in the story.

Create one sentence describing a change you observed in Almanzo since the beginning of the book.

<u>   Possible ideas might be that he is more responsible, reliable, more mature, more confident,</u>

<u>or that he is beginning to think seriously about his future.</u>

Setting: Setting means the <u>time</u> and <u>place</u> in which the story happens.

1. Write one sentence about a place in the story, other than the Wilders' farm. <u>   Ideas might   </u>

    <u>include the timber forest, Mr. Paddock's wagon shop, or the county fair.</u>

    _____

2. Write one sentence describing what Almanzo saw in Mr. Paddock's shop. Strong imagery (sights,

    sounds, smells) will improve your sentence. <u>   You may refer to page 353   </u>

    <u>(beginning with "It was warm in the building …").   Answers will vary.</u>

    _____

Plot: Plot means <u>action</u> or <u>what happens</u> in the story.

Write about the plot related to Almanzo finding and returning Mr. Thompson's pocketbook. Summarize the action that takes place. Use plenty of detail.

_____

_____

_____

_____

_____

_____

_____

_____

_____

_____

_____

Extra Practice

Drawing Page

Illustrate a scene from your favorite chapter of *Farmer Boy*.
Write the chapter title above your picture.

Title goes here

Vocabulary

Write the letter of the vocabulary word on the line in front of its definition.

1. ___x___ serving
2. ___o___ grouped
3. ___k___ struggled helplessly
4. ___m___ has a right to
5. ___l___ manners
6. ___w___ sharp
7. ___i___ cape
8. ___j___ to polish by scrubbing
9. ___n___ one who works for instruction
10. ___a___ pointed
11. ___p___ stuttered
12. ___d___ bound at one end w/ loose threads
13. ___s___ scissors
14. ___u___ hard, outer covering of grain
15. ___c___ to separate grain from chaff
16. ___e___ trampled; worn down
17. ___f___ in a calming manner
18. ___g___ strong
19. ___h___ held tightly
20. ___q___ chopped; carved
21. ___v___ lean
22. ___r___ thankful
23. ___b___ flexible
24. ___y___ to remove outer leaves
25. ___t___ shook violently

a. tapered
b. pliable
c. thresh
d. tasseled
e. trodden
f. soothingly
g. stout
h. clutched
i. cloak
j. scour
k. floundered
l. deportment
m. entitled
n. apprentice
o. clustered
p. stammered
q. hewed
r. obliged
s. shears
t. quaked
u. chaff
v. gaunt
w. keen
x. catering
y. husk

Quiz 3 Review

Short Answer
Answer the following questions in complete sentences.

1. What does the threat of a switch have to do with Almanzo's good behavior before Christmas? ____

    Switches or a trip to the woodshed means the same thing: a spanking. Almanzo behaves well to

    avoid this.

2. Give an example of how Almanzo has learned to use patience and gentleness in training his oxen.

    When his team begins to see-saw, he takes Joe's advice and speaks to them gently to settle them

    and get them to pull together. He speaks encouragingly to them when they make mistakes.

3. Why is Almanzo so angry with Mr. Thompson? _____ Almanzo is angry because Mr.

    Thompson called him a "durn boy" and implied that he was a thief.

4. Explain the difference between Mother's and Father's hopes for Almanzo's future. _____

    Mother wants him to be a farmer—no questions! She feels working a town job will keep him

    dependent on others for his living and won't produce character in a man as farming would. ("…

    but he'll never be the man you are.") Father wants him to be a farmer also, but he wants to be sure

    Almanzo clearly understands the options of both choices, and he thinks Almanzo should make his

    own decision.

5. What does Almanzo want more than anything in the world? How does he decide this? _____

    He wants to be like Father, free and independent. He knows he doesn't want to live inside walls

    and please people he doesn't like. He wants to own horses, cows, and fields.

Vocabulary Crosswords

Using the definitions below, choose the vocabulary word from the word bank to fit the puzzle.

Word Bank

placidly	sternly	shears	pliable	obliged
tapered	scour	inquiry	chaff	balk
sleek	briskly	impudently	hatchet	drowsy

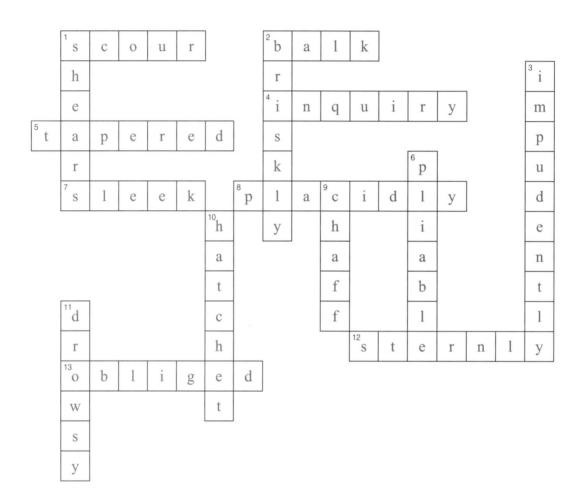

Across:

1. to polish by scrubbing
2. to stop short and refuse to go on
4. question
5. pointed
7. smooth; slick
8. calmly; peacefully
12. firmly; severely
13. thankful

Down:

1. scissors
2. quickly; with spirit
3. disrespectfully
6. flexible
9. hard, outer covering of grain
10. small, short-handled ax
11. sleepy

Vocabulary Crosswords

Using the definitions below, choose the vocabulary word from the word bank to fit the puzzle.

Word Bank

swathes	hustle	clutched	askew	term
trodden	aromatic	rousing	shrewd	dawdle
apprentice	soothingly	dappled	gritty	trudged

Across:

1. walked with heavy feet
7. bent to one side
9. sandy
11. to waste time; to be slow
13. held tightly
14. scented
15. crafty; clever

Down:

2. waking
3. spotted
4. sections, rows
5. one who works in return for instruction
6. grading period; semester
8. trampled; worn down
10. in a calming manner
12. hurry

Character Identification

Using the name bank, match each name to a description and write the name on the line.

| Mother | Mr. Thompson | Frank | Nick Brown | Mr. Paddock |
| Mr. Corse | Father | Almanzo | Eliza Jane | horse-buyer |

1. _____Frank_____ disobedient; dares Almanzo to do things

2. _____Father_____ his word is as good as his bond

3. _____Eliza Jane_____ bossy; always knows what is best to do

4. _____Mr. Corse_____ gentle and patient and never whips little boys

5. _____Almanzo_____ about nine years old; loves farming

6. _____Mother_____ short and plump and pretty

7. _____Mr. Paddock_____ a wheelwright; owner of the wagon shop

8. _____Mr. Thompson_____ suspicious of banks and selfish with his money

9. _____Nick Brown_____ a jolly, fat man who tells stories and sings songs

10. _____horse-buyer_____ wears city clothes, has black eyes, and a waxed mustache

Who Said That?

Using the name bank at the top of the page, match each name to a quotation and write the name on the line.

1. _____Almanzo_____ "I guess I know how to handle my own calves."

2. _____Eliza Jane_____ "It isn't the style to drink out of saucers anymore."

3. _____Father_____ "You're a good milker, son."

4. _____Mr. Paddock_____ "You ever think of making a wheelwright out of him?"

5. _____Mr. Corse_____ "Stay in at recess and learn it."

6. _____Frank_____ "I guess I'd do it if I wanted to, if I was you."

7. _____Mr. Thompson_____ "Well, this durn boy didn't steal any of it."

8. _____horse-buyer_____ "All right, two hundred it is. I'll lose money by it, but here you are."

9. _____Mother_____ "My butter speaks for itself."

10. _____Nick Brown_____ "I'll tell story for story and sing song for song …"

Multiple Choice

Choose the best answer for each question.

1. Why does Almanzo anxiously await the dark of the moon in May?

    a. It is time to plant crops, and he loves working in the fields with Father.

    b. It becomes warmer and he can stay outdoors longer.

    c. He can stay home from school and plant pumpkins.

2. Why does Almanzo's teacher stay with the Wilder family at their home?

    a. He is poor and has nowhere else to go.

    b. He likes their family the best of all the other families.

    c. Each family boards the teacher for two weeks, and it is the Wilders' turn.

3. Why don't the Wilders make their own shoes?

    a. They don't have the right quality of animal hide for shoes.

    b. Cobblers' work is highly skilled and requires special equipment.

    c. They are too busy farming and don't have time to make shoes.

4. On Independence Day, when Almanzo wants a nickel, why does Father ask him about potatoes?

    a. He wants him to understand how much work goes into earning money and to value it.

    b. Father wants to convince Almanzo not to buy lemonade.

    c. Father wants to impress his adult friend with Almanzo's farming knowledge.

5. What gifts does Almanzo receive from his parents for his birthday? **Both** must be true!

    a. a sled and warm, woolen mittens

    b. a small yoke for his ox calves and a sled

    c. a jack-knife and a yoke for his oxen

6. Why does Father show Almanzo how to make the sled rather than just make it all for him?

    a. Father wants him to learn the skills by doing it himself, and he knows that will also teach him to more deeply appreciate and take care of the sled.

    b. Father doesn't have the time to make it for him; Almanzo has to help or it won't get done.

    c. He wants Almanzo to be able to fix his sled by himself if it is ever broken.

7. What does Mr. Paddock discuss with Father?

    a. Mr. Paddock has no sons of his own and wants Almanzo to work for him as an apprentice.

    b. Mr. Paddock wants to ask Father's permission to recommend Almanzo to another farmer for a job.

    c. Mr. Paddock admires Almanzo's honesty and wants to say so to Father.

8. What does Almanzo like **best** about Saturdays, and what does he like **least**? **Both** must be true!

    a. no school / knowing that tomorrow he has to sit still all day

    (b.) baking day / taking a bath

    c. fewer chores on Saturday / taking a bath

9. Why is Father in a hurry to harvest the potatoes?

    a. He has so much other work to do for harvesting that is more important to get done.

    (b.) There is a threat of frost which will kill the potato crop.

    c. The family has no potatoes left to eat and they depend on them for food.

10. What makes Almanzo feel grown-up and important at the fair?

    a. He is allowed to leave his parents and spend time playing with his cousin.

    b. He knows the names of all the different types of horses, cows, and sheep at the fair.

    (c.) He feels important talking about horses with Father.

Short Answer
Answer the questions below in complete sentences.

1. Throughout most of the book, Father does not trust Almanzo around the colts. What does he fear will happen? _He knows that a young boy could easily do something that would spoil a colt, thus making them more difficult or impossible to train later._

2. Name and *briefly* describe TWO different salesmen that visit the Wilder farm. _Possible answers include the tin-peddler, the horse-buyer, the butter-buyer, and the cobbler._

3. The Wilders grow or make much of what they use for everyday living. List three things they need on a regular basis that they produce themselves on their farm. _Answers may include wool for cloth, other items of clothing, butter, most of their meat, vegetables and grain, candles, soap, sleds, some tools (i.e., flail), ice, and wood for heat and building._

4. Choose one of the following "lessons" that Almanzo learns as a child, and give an example from the book of how he learned or used this lesson. *(patience, the value of money, telling the truth)*

    Answers may include: **patience** - training the oxen, waiting to train the colt

    **value of money** - 50¢ on Independence Day, growing potatoes, buying the pig

    **telling the truth** - his milk-fed pumpkin, asking for money, Mr. Thompson's pocketbook

5. What does Father do at the end of the book that proves he thinks Almanzo is growing up? _____

   <u>He tells Almanzo he can have Starlight for his own to train.</u>
   _____

Paragraph
Answer the question below in 3-5 complete sentences.

Describe a farmer based on what you know after reading *Farmer Boy.*

<u>Answers will vary.</u>

_____

_____

_____

_____

_____

_____

_____

_____

_____

Appendix

Laura Ingalls Wilder

Laura Ingalls Wilder, author of the *Little House* series, was born February 7, 1867. She was the second of five children, having three surviving sisters and one brother who died in infancy. She was born near Pepin, Wisconsin, and her life there served as the basis for her book *Little House in the Big Woods.*

The Ingalls Family: seated from left Caroline (Laura's mother), Charles (Laura's father), Mary. Standing from left Carrie, Laura, Grace.

In Laura's early childhood, her father moved the family to Indian territory in Kansas, hoping to establish a homestead. This period of her life is recounted in *Little House on the Prairie*. In the following years, Pa Ingalls moved his family to Minnesota, Iowa, back to Minnesota, and finally to South Dakota where he, his wife, and daughter Mary remained for the rest of their lives.

Once the family was settled in DeSmet, South Dakota, Laura was able to attend school and eventually met her future husband, Almanzo Wilder. She accepted a teaching position at the age of 15, teaching in various one-room schools and continuing her own education as well. By her own admission, she never really enjoyed teaching, but did so to aid her family financially.

On August 28, 1885, Laura Ingalls and "Manly" Wilder were married, at which time Laura quit teaching. Despite a promising beginning, she and Almanzo (see left) experienced many difficulties during their life together, both physically and financially. Through hard work, determination, and some outside help, they were able to eventually establish a prosperous farm in Mansfield, Missouri, called Rocky Ridge Farm. They remained at this farm until their deaths, Almanzo in 1949 at the age of ninety-two, and Laura in 1957 at the age of ninety.

A 19th Century Primer

Many different kinds of primers have been published and used throughout the years in the United States. Perhaps the two best known are The New England Primer and McGuffey Readers.

The New England Primer

This teaching text was first published between 1687 and 1690 by a man named Benjamin Harris. It was the first reading primer to be published in the American Colonies and became the most widely used textbook in the early days of America. It consisted of the alphabet, vowels, consonants, and various two-to-six letter syllables. Reading was taught primarily through the use of short religious prayers and poetry, wood cut pictures, and moral lessons. Some versions of this text also included a short catechism. Respect for one's parents, sin, and salvation were common themes.

During this early period of history, other, more secular, primers were also written but did not stay in use for long. The alphabet, however, remained the common systematic means of introducing reading and spelling to young children.

McGuffey Readers

These enduring classics were originally written by William Holmes McGuffey and first published in 1836-1837. They were written as a set of four readers, each one progressing in difficulty from the previous. They used word repetition as a learning tool.

The first Reader used the phonics method and focused on identifying letters, simple words, and writing practice (done on a slate). Once a child had mastered these beginning skills of reading, he moved into the second Reader. This taught him to understand the meaning of sentences and provided vivid stories and lessons that could be easily remembered. The third Reader taught advanced skills and definitions of words, while the fourth, and final, Reader aimed at the highest level of learning in the grammar school.

The earliest primers taught vocabulary through lists that were simply memorized. But McGuffey introduced a new style of presenting vocabulary, by using it within the context of a real story. He believed teachers should study the lessons with their students (instead of the student merely memorizing and reciting them) and encouraged reading aloud to the class. He also believed that asking questions was an important tool of teaching, and included questions at the end of each lesson.

The content of the earliest McGuffey Readers offered a curriculum rich in religious beliefs and manners. But as with the New England primers before, revised editions did not contain the same forthright values of salvation and piety. The content of the Readers became more focused on simply being a good person and treating others well. However, McGuffey himself neither wrote these revisions nor approved their content.

McGuffey Readers have declined in use over the years, but have not entirely disappeared. They are still in use today, especially within the homeschool movement.

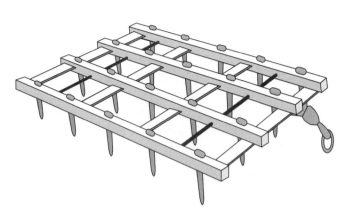

harrow:

A harrow was used for the preparation of the soil before planting. It served to smooth out rough, clumpy soil to ensure that crops could be planted evenly. Iron spikes were attached to a wooden frame and the frame was then pulled behind horses. The harrow pictured here was used in areas that were already free of large obstacles such as tree stumps.

plow:

During the 1800's, a plow was the most important piece of farming equipment. It was used to break up and turn the soil before planting a crop. With a plow such as the one pictured here, a whole day was needed to plow only 1-2 acres of land! Plows were expensive, and most farmers could not afford to own one. Therefore, farmers who were fortunate enough to own a plow often loaned it to their surrounding neighbors in exchange for labor or goods.

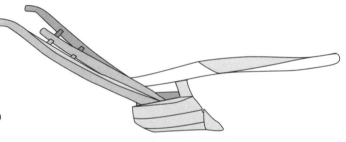

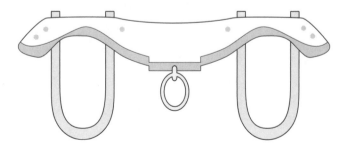

yoke:

This is a straight yoke, the most common kind used for oxen. The large wooden bar was fitted on the back of the oxen's necks while the U-shaped bows were fitted under the neck and were attached with iron pins. A plow or wagon could be attached to the large iron ring in the middle of the yoke.

flail:

This was a tool used for threshing grain. It was made of a long wooden handle attached with leather loops to a shorter stick. The grain was laid out on the floor of a barn and the thresher would swing the handle of the flail in a circular motion— first down, back, then around and over the head. As it continued around and down, the shorter stick would swing freely, striking the grain. As it was beaten, the kernels of grain would separate from the husk and fall through the straw to the floor. The straw was then carefully lifted, and the grain was collected and stored.

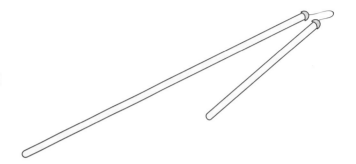

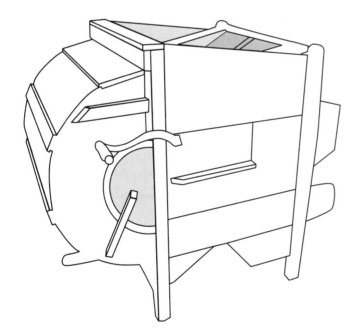

fanning-mill:

This tool was used to separate wheat grain from the chaff (garbage). The harvested grain was shoveled into the "hopper" on top while the handle was turned. As the fans worked inside the mill, chaff was blown out the front of the machine. The kernels of clean wheat came out and were collected on another side.

scythe:

A scythe was used primarily for cutting grass or reaping crops. In Almanzo's day, they were usually made from wood, having a straight shaft with a short grip and a curved metal blade. Mowing with a scythe is done by holding the top handle with the left hand and the central grip in the right hand. The arms remain straight and the blade stays parallel and close to the ground. As a person cuts, the body twists to the left in a steady rhythm. As the grain is cut, it falls in rows, called swathes, on the ground, to be gathered later.

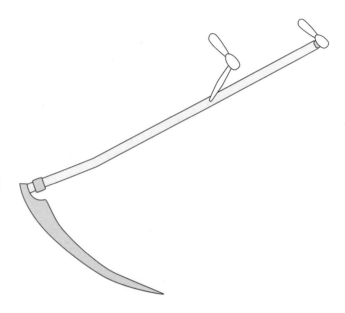

hay press:

The hay press (or as the book indicates, also known as a "railroad press") was an early form of the hay-baler and was used to bundle hay in order to make it easier for transport. They came into use around the middle of the 1800's, but were not used regularly by the average farmer until the 1870's. The fact that the Wilders used one speaks of their wealth and progressive farming practices. It was a stationary machine powered by a horse. The box chamber was filled with hay, and as the horse walked in a circular motion, it set in action gears and a chain drive that compressed the hay tightly. It was then manually tied together with twine, wire, or, as in the book, ash-withes, which were strips of pliable tree bark.

A man's "waist."

A woman's "hoop skirt."

A woman's "basque."

Birds' Nest Pudding

Brown sugar baked in green apples, nested in a pastry crust
(as referred to in *Farmer Boy*, "Filling the Ice-House")

Ingredients:

6	green apples; tart, peeled, cored		1 cup	flour
1	cup brown sugar		1 tsp	cream of tartar
¼ tsp	nutmeg		½ tsp	baking powder
3	egg whites		½ tsp	salt
3	egg yolks			
1 cup	whole milk		Sweetened Cream:	
1 tsp	maple flavoring		½ cup	powdered sugar
			¼ tsp	nutmeg
			1 pint	heavy whipping cream

Directions:

1. **Preheat oven** to 350° F. Prepare a buttered 2-quart baking dish.

2. **Prepare the apples**: Place apples in baking dish. Fill each apple with brown sugar, pressing slightly. Save any unused sugar. Sprinkle nutmeg over the apples. Place dish in oven to begin baking as batter is prepared.

3. **Prepare the batter**: Beat the egg whites until stiff. In a separate bowl, beat the egg yolks until they change color. Add milk and maple flavoring to the yolks. In another separate bowl, mix the flour, cream of tartar, baking powder, salt, and the remaining brown sugar until well blended. Pour the flour mixture all together into the yolk mixture, stirring until blended. Fold the beaten egg whites into the blended flour and yolks. This batter will be thin.

4. **Combine apples and batter**: Remove apples from oven and pour batter into the baking dish, over and around the apples evenly. Return the dish to the oven and bake another 45 to 60 minutes.

5. **Prepare the cream**: Stir powdered sugar and nutmeg into the heavy cream.

6. Remove dish from oven when crust is lightly browned. Before it falls, quickly and carefully turn each apple along with some surrounding crust onto a plate, so the apple is nested in the crust. Top with sweetened cream.

The Hayloft

Through all the pleasant meadow-side
The grass grew shoulder-high,
Till the shining scythes went far and wide
And cut it down to dry.

These green and sweetly smelling crops
They led in wagons home;
And they piled them here in mountain tops
For mountaineers to roam.

Here is Mount Clear, Mount Rusty-Nail,
Mount Eagle and Mount High;—
The mice that in these mountains dwell,
No happier are than I!

O what a joy to clamber there,
O what a place for play,
With the sweet, the dim, the dusty air,
The happy hills of hay!

The Happy Farmer

Let the mighty and great
Roll in splendor and state,
I envy them not, I declare it.
I eat my own lamb,
My own chicken and ham;
I shear my own sheep and I wear it.

I have lawns and green bowers,
Fresh fruits and fine flowers,
The lark is my bright morning charmer.
So God bless the plow
In the future as now—
A health and long life to the farmer.

Discussion Questions
Answer Key

Discussion questions that have a * are NECESSARY to discuss with students as they may appear on a test and are generally important in understanding the full flavor of the story.

Lesson 1: School Days

1. *Find the title page of the book, then turn the page to see publishing information. In what year did Laura Ingalls Wilder write *Farmer Boy*? Based on this knowledge and the first paragraph of the chapter, figure out the year in which the story is set. Where does the story take place?

   The story is set in the year 1866. The story takes place in New York state.

2. Locate New York state on a U.S. map. What would the weather be like in that part of the country?

   The weather would be cold and snowy during the winter.

3. Why does Mr. Corse give the Hardscrabble boys another chance after they are tardy?

   Mr. Corse is patient. He may want more time to think about how to handle these difficult boys or to get advice from Mr. Wilder. He wants to create a situation where the boys have been clearly warned and then obviously disobeyed him so the punishment won't be unfair in any way.

4. Explain the seating arrangement in the classroom. What do you think is the purpose of this arrangement?

   Girls sit on the left side of the room, boys sit on the right side. Older children sit in the back, younger children sit in front. The purpose is to group them according to age, size, and skill.

Lesson 2: Winter Evening

1. *The first quote above describes Father. According to it and other statements in the chapter, what kind of a man is he? What does the author mean by saying, "His word was as good as his bond"? From this chapter, how can you tell he is a good father to his children?

   Father is a big man. He is serious. He is hard-working and thrifty. He is wealthy. He has a sense of humor (his eyes twinkle). He thinks ahead and makes decisions carefully (he won't let Almanzo touch the colts until he proves he is trustworthy). He doesn't speak unless he has something worthwhile to say. "His word is as good as his bond" means that Father is honest. His word is a good as a written promise. He is a good father because he expects obedience from his children. He compliments Almanzo on his job of milking. He gives his sons work to do that he knows they can handle well. He teaches his sons by showing them how to do things.

2. *Why doesn't Father trust Almanzo around the colts? What does he fear will happen, and how does Almanzo feel about this?

   Father knows that young, unbroken horses are easily spoiled. If a careless boy scares or strikes a colt it can make it difficult or impossible to train well later. Almanzo feels misjudged; he can be trusted around the colts and knows how to act around them.

3. In the second quote above, the cold is described as being cruel. What does that mean? How does that phrase help you understand how Almanzo is feeling at that moment?

   "The cold is cruel" means that the air is harsh and almost unbearably cold. The phrase helps you imagine the bitter cold in contrast to the warmth of the kitchen that Almanzo can't wait to enter.

Lesson 3: Winter Night

1. What chores does the family do immediately after supper?

   Almanzo and Royal grease their moccasins and boots. Mother and the girls clean up the kitchen. Father goes to the cellar to cut up vegetables to feed the cows.

2. Find the pages that describe the Wilders' breakfast. What do they eat? Why do you think Mother cooks so much variety for this meal?

> The Wilders eat pancakes, sausage, gravy, oatmeal with cream, fried potatoes, doughnuts, and pies. Their daily work is hard and physical, so they need a hearty meal for energy to get them through the morning.

Lesson 4: Surprise

1. *In the quote above, what is Father saying about Mr. Corse?

> Father means that Mr. Corse is an honorable man, who is aware of the danger he faces from the Hardscrabble boys, but who will courageously face that danger and do the right thing to take care of the problem.

2. Why does Mr. Corse focus on Big Bill instead of dealing with any of the other big boys first?

> He focuses on Big Bill because he is the leader and the other boys will follow his example.

3. What virtues does Mr. Corse display in the way he disciplines Big Bill?

> Mr. Corse is strong, courageous, and firm. He keeps his word by doing what he says he will do. He is just; he doesn't let them get by with wrong behavior just because they are bigger and stronger. He defends himself and protects the students.

Lesson 5: Birthday

1. *Read the first quote above. The book says Almanzo feels he is now old enough to do important things by himself. Why? Why do you think Father stops helping him and goes into the barn?

> Almanzo knows he is old enough to do important things because Father leaves him alone to figure out how to train the oxen. Almanzo is now 9 years old. Father is giving him more responsibility and a chance to show he can handle it.

2. Explain how Almanzo teaches Star and Bright to understand "Giddap" and "Whoa."

> He uses carrots to entice them to move forward as he says, "Giddap." When they stop to eat he says, "Whoa."

3. While Almanzo is watching Mother work, she tells him she is making a suit for Royal that he will need next winter. Why will it take her so long to make this suit?

> Mother is now weaving the cloth for Royal's suit. When that is done she will still need to cut out the pieces of the suit and sew it together. Besides this, she has lots of other work to do every day, so she has to plan ahead in order to make sure the clothing will be finished in time.

4. Compare and contrast Almanzo's birthday with your own birthday celebration.

> Almanzo does not go to school on his birthday. He does his regular chores and receives only a couple gifts. We generally have a party with our friends that includes a special cake, special decorations, cards and gifts, and singing the "Happy Birthday" song. Like Almanzo, we usually spend time with our parents and/or other relatives, and have extra play time of some kind.

Discussion Questions Answer Key   **95**

Lesson 6: Filling the Ice-House

1. Read the first quote. What is the punchline of the "flip a penny" joke? Why is it about Irishmen, not Frenchmen?

> The punchline is "Who goes below?" Obviously, no one can go below the ice under water to use the other end of the saw. The joke is about Irishmen because they are French and wouldn't make fun of a Frenchman's confusion or misunderstanding.

2. What would have happened if Almanzo had actually fallen in the ice?

> He would have been drawn under the solid ice by the water's current. Noboby would be able to find him and he would drown.

3. Why do you think sawdust is used to cover the top layer of ice and to fill the cracks?

> Sawdust is readily available to them and it is good natural insulation.

4. How do the Wilders use the ice they store in the summer months?

> They use the stored ice blocks to make ice cream (Ch. 18), lemonade, and egg-nog (Ch. 19).

Lesson 7: Saturday Night

1. How does Mother make doughnuts? What is special about her doughnuts?

> Mother rolls out the dough and then fries her doughnuts in hot fat. She twists her doughnuts so they will turn themselves over.

2. The Wilders' bath procedure is involved. What other chores were more difficult then?

> Traveling was more difficult. It also took more time and work to get ice, candles, butter, all of their clothing, and even water. They had to make many items that we can simply buy or don't use anymore (i.e., shingles, yokes, sleds, cloth)

3. What bedtime clothing does Almanzo put on after his bath? Why must he dress so warmly?

> Almanzo puts on a warm underwaist, woolly long drawers, a long woolen nightshirt, socks, and a cap. They use wood to warm the house, but the fire will not burn as strong and hot during the night. Therefore they need extra layers of clothing to stay warm.

Lesson 8: Sunday

1. "Every man who belonged to the church paid rent for a shed, according to his means, and Father had the best one." What does the phrase "according to his means" mean? What does this say about Father?

> "According to his means" means the amount of money the person can afford to pay. Since Father has the best shed, it means he is a wealthy man compared to others in the town.

2. *Farmer Boy* includes many detailed descriptions of food. Why do you think this is?

> The book often speaks of food perhaps because their life is relatively simple and food is a major enjoyable part of it. The story is told from the viewpoint of a nine-year-old boy, and young boys are active and growing and usually enjoy eating.

3. What are Almanzo's thoughts about his cousin Frank's "store-boughten" cap? Based on what Royal says, how does Almanzo know he wants a cap like that too?

> Almanzo likes the cap and wants to have one of his own, but he knows they are expensive and his parents wouldn't "waste" money on something he doesn't need. He knows Royal wants one too because Royal criticizes it and pretends so hard that he doesn't want one.

4. Consider the way in which the Wilders traveled. Contrast the differences between their means of travel and how you travel.

> Answers will vary. Answers may include that the Wilders travel primarily by foot or by horse and open buggy. We travel by many means, including foot, car, train, airplane, bus, and bicycle.

Lesson 9: Breaking the Calves

1. Based on the first quote above, why does Almanzo not whip Star and Bright even when they are not obeying?

> He knows that an animal will never learn anything if he whips it. He has to be patient. He knows that if he elevates his degree of punishment, the oxen might increase their tolerance for that punishment. If he wants them to respond to a stern voice, he needs to be consistent in training them to respond to it.

2. Read the second quote. Why does Almanzo say this? Judging from the outcome of his "splendid idea," do you agree with this statement? Why or why not?

> Almanzo is defending his decision to leave the barnyard with the oxen because Pierre questioned the wisdom of what he was doing. Answers may vary.

Lesson 10: The Turn of the Year

1. Explain the first quote above.

> Just after the winter solstice (Dec. 21) the days slowly begin to get longer again. However, the coldest and harshest part of winter (January and February) is yet to come.

2. Explain how maple syrup and maple sugar are made.

> [See explanation, pages 110-112] Father bores a hole in the maple tree, fitted with a spout. The sap drips into buckets that are collected and poured into a large caldron. The liquid is boiled for most of a day. Then the syrup is done. To make sugar Mother boils the syrup longer on the cook-stove until it is ready to "sugar off." It is then poured into a pan and allowed to cool into a solid cake.

Lesson 11: Springtime

1. The third paragraph of this chapter describes the work horses. Explain the phrase "wise, sober mares."

> The mares are mature work horses, older than Almanzo and experienced in field work. They aren't wild and frisky like the colts.

2. The first quote above describes Almanzo as a soldier in a battle. What is the battle, and in what way is he like a soldier in this battle?

> The battle is against the weeds, to keep them from overgrowing the good plants. Almanzo is a soldier in the sense that he helps fight the weeds by working hard to get the good seeds planted before the weeds have a chance to grow.

3. Describe how the potatoes are planted.

> They cut seed potatoes so each piece that would be planted has two or three eyes. Next, they drop one piece in every marked corner on the grid of furrows Father has made. The potato seeds are then covered with dirt.

Discussion Questions Answer Key   **97**

Lesson 12: Tin-Peddler

1. Think back to the types of wares the peddler brings. Does your family use any of these items? Are there items he sells that we don't use at all anymore?

> We still use items such as pails, pans, cups, dippers, strainers, colanders, and graters, but they are no longer made of tin. Most are made of plastic or stainless steel. We no longer make toys out of tin.

2. What would the life of a peddler be like? Would it be an adventure or a chore? Why?

> The life of a peddler could be an adventure because you would experience different places and people. You could make friends with many people. Each day would be different; you wouldn't have much routine. It could also be a chore because you'd have to work hard all winter to have items to sell. You'd depend on others for your needs, have times of loneliness while traveling, and possibly encounter difficult situations. You'd spend a lot of time away from your family.

3. What kinds of people might a peddler meet on his journeys?

> A peddler would meet all kinds of people. Some may be friendly and hospitable, while others may be unfriendly and unkind. He may also encounter dishonest or dangerous people.

Lesson 13: The Strange Dog

1. *In what small way does Father acknowledge that Almanzo is becoming more trustworthy around the young horses?

> Father allows Almanzo to help groom the four-year-old colts to get them ready for the horse-buyer.

2. How is Father's bargaining with the horse-buyer similar to Mother's trading for tin-ware?

> Father purposely asks the horse-buyer for more money than he is willing to accept, in order to get a higher price for his horses.

3. Why do you think Mother hears the noise in the middle of the night, but Father sleeps soundly?

> Mother was nervous about having so much money in the house, but Father was sure they would be safe. Because Mother was worried, she doesn't sleep very well that night and therefore is easily awakened when she hears the dog outside, growling.

Lesson 14: Sheep-Shearing

1. Why do the men wash the sheep in the river instead of in tubs? Why are they washed before shearing instead of afterwards?

> It is easier to wash the sheep in the flowing river instead of constantly needing to fill and empty a tub. It is also easier while it is still on the sheep. Once sheared, the wool is then ready to store.

2. Why do you think Father laughs and says Almanzo can't keep up with the others after he has just sternly told him to do so? Do his words have the desired effect?

> Father is trying to motivate and challenge Almanzo to work harder by suggesting that he can't do the job. Yes, they have the desired effect. Almanzo determines to show them that he can do it.

Discussion Questions Answer Key

3. Why does Father think Almanzo's joke on Lazy John is so funny?

> He thinks it is funny that a young boy like Almanzo can be clever enough to play a better joke on an adult. When two people try to play a joke on each other, the person who has the last laugh (or the one who triumphs) enjoys the joke the most.

4. Explain why sheep are so important to the Wilder family.

> The Wilders use the sheep's wool to make their clothing.

Lesson 15: Cold Snap

1. Explain Mother's process for soap-making.

> She saves all the wood ashes throughout the winter and puts them in a barrel. Water is poured over them and the resulting lye is allowed to drip out of a hole in the bottom of the barrel. Mother measures some of the lye into a caldron. She adds pork rinds together with pork and beef fat and boils this mixture until brown, slimy soap forms. This soft-soap is skimmed out and put into tubs.

2. What is meant by the sentence "The sun was coming to kill the corn"?

> If the sun warmed the frozen plants too quickly, they would die. The cold water allows for a more gradual warming instead of a shock that will kill them. The sun is rising suddenly, and the Wilders aren't yet finished with their task.

3. Reread the two quotes above. Why do you think the Wilders are able to save most of the corn even though there are thousands of hills of it and they don't start working until the middle of the night? Why is it so important to them to save it?

> The entire family works together to get the job done before sunrise. They know it is vital to get to every hill of corn, so they all work as hard as they can even though they are cold, tired, and hungry. It is important because the crops on the farm provide cash income as well as feed for their livestock.

Lesson 16: Independence Day

1. Explain how Independence Day is celebrated in the town of Malone. What are the main events during the celebration?

> People dress in their Sunday best clothes. The town has flags posted, contests, music, public speakers, reading of the Declaration of Independence, picnics, a parade, and the firing of the brass cannon.

2. How do Frank and Mr. Paddock respond similarly in this chapter?

> Frank doesn't believe Father will give Almanzo money if he asks for it, so he dares him to try. Mr. Paddock thinks Almanzo is too young to understand the value of money. Although he doesn't actually dare Father to make him understand, his facial expression is like a challenge to Father.

3. Using the second quote above, explain Father's earlier statement: "It was axes and plows that made this country."

> Father explains that although many people came to America to make quick money, it was the farmers who worked long and hard to settle the land and live there. Their willingness to work hard for a good cause made America a strong nation.

Discussion Questions Answer Key

Lesson 17: Summer-Time

1. *What does Father teach Almanzo about growing pumpkins? Explain the process.

   He cuts a slit in the pumpkin vine and sticks a candle wick into it. The other end of the wick is placed in a pan of milk. The milk is wicked up into the vine and consumed by the growing pumpkin, causing it to grow faster and larger than it would simply by consuming liquid from the vine through natural process.

2. Explain the second quote above.

   Good mental health requires a balance between work and play. If a person works too much and never takes time for rest and refreshment he may become dull of spirit and less effective in his work.

3. Describe the family berrying excursion and Almanzo's surprise encounter.

   The family piles into the wagon with a picnic and buckets and goes to the mountains near a lake. Other families are berrying there, too. They pick blueberries and huckleberries all day, eat their picnic, and have fun. Almanzo's surprise is encountering a bear in the woods.

Lesson 18: Keeping House

1. What does Almanzo do as soon as he thinks no one is watching him? What happens?

   He steals into the pasture where the colts are. As he slowly moves closer to them, the bigger colts suddenly begin to stampede right toward him. He can't get out of the way in time, and as they pass him, one even jumps over him. He feels stunned.

2. What do Alice and Almanzo do in the parlor? Why do they hide their activity from Eliza Jane?

   They play on the slippery furniture, giggling and sliding. They don't want Eliza Jane to know because they know she will be angry and make them leave. She would probably also tell Mother on them later.

3. How does Almanzo's guilty conscience punish him when the Webbs come to visit?

   He is worried that the stain he has caused on the parlor wall will embarrass Mother. He is also fearful of the sure punishment that will follow its discovery.

4. Based on the entire chapter and the quotes above, is Eliza Jane a good sister to Almanzo? Why or why not?

   Answers will vary. Possible answers: No, because she is so bossy and mean to him. Yes, she is bossy because she is trying to obey Mother by looking after the house and younger children. She also apologizes and covers Almanzo's mistake.

Lesson 19: Early Harvest

1. Explain Lazy John's words when he says, "That puts heart into a man!"

   He means that the egg-nog and a short break give him renewed energy for work.

2. Name all the work that must be done during the early harvest time.

   The hay must be cut and stored in the hay mow. Many of the crops are ready to be harvested: oats, wheat, beans, pumpkins, carrots, turnips, and potatoes. They make pickles and preserves. They also dry corn and apples.

Discussion Questions Answer Key

3. Describe the butter-buyer's visit. Why does Mother make a trip to town afterwards? Why is this unusual?

> The butter-buyer is from New York and always brings the latest news. When he tests Mother's butter with his long, thin tube with a slit down one side, he says it is the best butter anywhere. He pays her the enormous amount of $.50 per pound. She earns a total of $250. She makes a trip to town to put the money in the bank. This is unusual because usually she is too busy during the harvest to leave the farm.

Lesson 20: Late Harvest

1. Which crops are stored in the cellar? in the barn? in the attic? How is each type of food used?

> Food stored in the cellar: apples, the best pumpkins, turnips, parsnips, beets, cider, carrots, potatoes. Food stored in the barn: pumpkins used to feed the animals, corn shocks, beans. Food stored in the attic: onions, red peppers. The imperfect pumpkins and carrots are used to feed the animals. The rest of the crops are eaten by the Wilders.

2. What does Mother mean when she says, "A miss is as good as a mile"?

> The Wilder family barely saves the potatoes from frost. Mother means that if you avoid danger by a little bit (a miss), it is just as good as avoiding danger by a mile. You are safe either way.

Lesson 21: County Fair

1. *Why does the county fair take place after all the crops are harvested?

> If the fair had taken place earlier, no one would have been able to attend because they were all too busy harvesting their crops. They also would not have had mature produce to enter in the contests at the fair.

2. Explain what Father means when he says: "Never bet your money on another man's game."

> Father is teaching Almanzo that a game that is controlled by someone else will likely only be profitable for the person in control.

3. Describe the horse race. Why doesn't Father believe in betting on a winner?

> It is an exciting race. The horses run, pulling their sulkies so fast it is hard to see them. An Indian joins the race, running behind the pack of horses as fast as they run. Some people even bet on him! Father doesn't like to bet on a winner because the winning isn't guaranteed and he would rather get something of lasting value for his money.

Lesson 22: Fall of the Year

1. What is "poor man's fertilizer"? Why is snow plowed into unfrozen ground valuable?

> "Poor man's fertilizer" is an early winter snow that falls before the ground is frozen. This is valuable for farming because the snow contains nitrogen and sulphur which are naturally lacking in the soil.

2. How are the Wilders like the squirrels that are busy storing nuts for the winter?

> The Wilders work diligently preparing and storing food and other items they will need to live comfortably during the cold winter months, like squirrels.

3. Explain how butchering is done.

They kill the animal, dip the carcass into boiling water, scrape off the hair, hang it up by the hind feet in a tree, cut it open, and remove the insides. Then they skin the hide and cut and store the meat. They also make mincemeat, headcheese, and sausage.

4. What is headcheese? What is mincemeat? Use the book to find your answers.

Headcheese is the substance obtained from boiling the heads of the cattle and hogs. The meat is boiled off the bones; it is then chopped, seasoned, and mixed with water from the boiling. When cooled it forms a jelly-like substance that can be eaten. Mincemeat is boiled bits of beef and pork, chopped fine and mixed with raisins, spices, sugar, vinegar, chopped apples, and brandy. It is later made into pies.

Lesson 23: Cobbler

1. *What is the significance of Father's announcement that Almanzo's boots should be made first?

Father wants to cheer Almanzo up because his siblings have all gone to school. It is also Father's way of saying he recognizes that Almanzo is getting older and doing more "grown-up" work, which requires boots.

2. This chapter describes some of the common tools used and the process of shoe making. Using the context of the story, try to answer the following questions: What is a *last*? What is a *vise*, and how is it used? What is an *awl*? What is a *rasp*? What does it mean to "bore a hole"?

last: a block or form shaped like a human foot and used in making/repairing shoes

vise: a clamping tool used to hold something in place

awl: a sharp, pointed tool used for making holes in wood or leather

rasp: a coarse file with sharp pointed projections

bore a hole: to make a hole, formed by digging, drilling, or burrowing

Lesson 24: The Little Bobsled

1. Read the quotations above. What imagery does the author use to describe the snow? What is seen? What is heard? What is felt? To what are the snowflakes and the wind compared?

The author uses the imagery of feathers, a veil, and someone crying to describe the snow.

Seen: trees, feathery flakes

Heard: the sound of flakes falling, the lonely sound of the wind "crying"

Felt: whirling wind, heavy milk-pails

The snowflakes are being compared to light, floating feathers. The wind is being compared to the crying of a lonely person.

2. What specific kinds of trees are needed to build the bobsled?

They need straight, small oak trees, two small crooked trees about the same size, and an elm sapling.

3. Describe the little bobsled, using as many details as you can.

> The bobsled has long, flat, smooth, curved runners, sturdy beams for cross-pieces, and two long, flat slabs on top as the base, attached by stout wooden pegs. At the front end is a "tongue" with an iron spike at the end, which will attach it to the oxen's yoke. Finally, it has four tall, wooden stakes to hold the logs in place while hauling.

Lesson 25: Threshing

1. Describe how Father and Almanzo thresh grain. How is the flail used?

> The flail is used to beat the grain free from the chaff and stalks. Father and Almanzo stand facing each other on opposite sides of a pile of grain. They then take turns hitting the grain with their flails. Once this is done, it is put into the fanning-mill where the chaff is blown apart from the good grains of wheat. It is then shoveled into large sacks and stored.

2. What is Almanzo likely to become when he grows up? What evidence supports your idea?

> Answers may vary. Almanzo is likely to become a farmer when he grows up. Throughout the book, so far, Almanzo is portrayed as a boy who much prefers the work of farming over book-learning in school. He loves working with and training the farm animals, especially looking forward to the day when he is allowed to train the horses.

3. Is there a place that feels completely comfortable and familiar to you? Why?

> Answers will vary.

Lesson 26: Christmas

1. What gifts does Almanzo receive? Why are these "practical" gifts so important to him?

> Almanzo receives a plaid boughten cap, horehound candy, new mittens, an orange, a package of dried figs, and a jack-knife with four blades. They are special because he does not expect them at all and rarely receives gifts.

2. Why is anticipation sometimes both wonderful and difficult at the same time?

> Waiting can be exciting as you look forward to what is about to happen. It can also be hard to wait for something that you know you will really enjoy and want right now.

3. Name some of the foods Mother serves at Christmas dinner. Why does Almanzo think the adults are heartless?

> The table holds roast pig and goose, dressing, cranberry jelly, potatoes, turnips, squash, parsnips, apples'n'onions, carrots, and pie. Almanzo feels that the adults are heartless because he is so hungry, yet they are enjoying getting their food before the children are served.

4. Christmas traditions can vary from family to family as well as from culture to culture. Compare and contrast the Wilders' Christmas traditions with those of your own family.

> The Wilders' celebration centers mostly around spending time with their extended family. They exchange gifts but they are few and practical. They travel in a sleigh and eat goose and pork. We spend time with our extended family as well, and many people attend special church services. We typically receive many presents, we travel by car or airplane, and we usually eat turkey or ham. The similar traditions between the Wilders and current traditions might be that children usually get up very early, before their parents, to check their stockings, and we visit with extended family, and we feast.

Lesson 27: Wood-Hauling

1. Explain how logs are lifted onto the bobsleds to be hauled back to the farm.

    > They use skids and cant-poles to roll the logs onto the sled. If the boys don't have cant-poles, they have to lift and push the logs up with their own strength.

2. What does Father do the first time he notices Almanzo struggling with his oxen in the ditch? What does he do the second time it happens? Why?

    > The first time he sees him in the ditch, "Father turned and watched, while he went by." He does not stop to try to help him, rather he lets Almanzo work it out himself. The second time, Father helps to untangle the oxen and get his sled back on the runners. He also helps him reload all the logs that have fallen off the sled. But from there on, he only watches and lets Almanzo do the rest by himself. When Almanzo is situated again, Father speaks encouraging words to him: "That's the way, son!" "Down again, up again!" He helps Almanzo the second time so that he won't get too discouraged because of his mistakes. He helps him just enough to get him back on track, then lets him try again on his own, knowing that this will build his confidence.

Lesson 28: Mr. Thompson's Pocketbook

1. What does Father mean when he says, "Many a good beginning makes a bad ending"?

    > Father means that many things that begin well may end badly. You can't make assumptions about the future outcome of some situations.

2. Mr. Case says, "I'd rather have a nimble sixpence than a slow shilling." What are sixpence and shillings? Explain the statement.

    > "Sixpence" and "shilling" are old forms of British money. Sixpence was a coin worth six pennies. A shilling was a coin worth 12 pence. Mr. Case would rather have many customers spending a small amount each, and who keep coming back, than just a few customers spending a large amount now and then.

3. *What does Almanzo mean when he gives the nickel back and says, "I can't change it."? Why is he so angry at Mr. Thompson?

    > Almanzo implies that Mr. Thompson is so stingy, he'd want change back for the nickel he'd given him as a "reward." Almanzo is angry because Mr. Thompson called him a "durn boy" and implied that he was a thief.

4. Reread the last two paragraphs of the chapter. What is Almanzo already planning to do with his money? Why is this exciting for the reader? How does the last line increase your desire to read on to the next chapter?

    > Almanzo is planning to buy a young colt that he can raise and train all by himself. This is exciting for the reader because the entire book has shown how much he loves horses and looks forward to the time he is old enough to work with them. Now, he finally has the means to do so! The last line increases our desire to read on because it promises an even more exciting outcome than we have already read. How else might Almanzo's hopes and dreams be realized?

Lesson 29: Farmer Boy

1. *Compare and contrast Mother's and Father's hopes for Almanzo's future.

   Mother wants him to be a farmer—no questions! She feels working a town job will keep him dependent on others for his living and won't produce character in a man as farming would. ("… but he'll never be the man you are.") Father wants him to be a farmer also, but he wants to be sure Almanzo clearly understands the options of both choices, and he thinks Almanzo should make his own decision.

2. *Father is fair and honest with Almanzo about his options. How does he explain city life? How does he explain farm life?

   Father explains that city life would be easier in some ways. He wouldn't have to be out in all kinds of weather, rain or shine, warm or cold. He'd be inside most of the time. He would have plenty to eat and money in the bank. As a farmer he would depend on himself, the land, and the weather. He would provide for himself food, clothing, and wood for warmth. He would work hard, but he'd be free and independent.

3. After reading *Farmer Boy*, what do you find appealing about farm life?

   Answers will vary.

Quizzes
&
Final Test

(reproducible for classroom use)

Farmer Boy Quiz 1

Chapters 1-10

Name _____

Date _____

Write the letter of the vocabulary word on the line in front of its definition.

1. _____ walked with heavy feet
2. _____ calmly; peacefully
3. _____ waking
4. _____ disrespectfully
5. _____ smooth; slick
6. _____ quickly; with spirit
7. _____ small, short-handled ax
8. _____ sleepy
9. _____ bent to one side
10. _____ scented

a. rousing
b. briskly
c. placidly
d. hatchet
e. impudently
f. drowsy
g. trudged
h. askew
i. sleek
j. aromatic

Match each name below with a character description.

Mother	Pierre and Louis	Frank	Father	Alice
Mr. Corse	Hardscrabble boys	Almanzo	Eliza Jane	Star and Bright

1. _____ bossy; always knows what is best to do

2. _____ just starting school; almost nine years old

3. _____ big, rough boys; everyone is afraid of them

4. _____ young oxen in need of "breaking"

5. _____ short, plump, and pretty; has blue eyes and brown hair

6. _____ races with Almanzo to fill potato baskets for town

7. _____ has a "store-boughten" cap that Almanzo admires

8. _____ gentle, patient, and never whips little boys

9. _____ stern, but has eyes that often twinkle

10. _____ live in the woods and never have to go to school

1. Why does Almanzo's teacher stay with the Wilder family at their home?

   a. He is poor and has nowhere else to go.

   b. He likes their family the best of all the other families.

   c. Each family boards the teacher for two weeks, and it is the Wilders' turn.

2. What gifts does Almanzo receive from his parents for his birthday? **Both** must be true!

   a. a sled and warm, woolen mittens

   b. a small yoke for his ox calves and a sled

   c. a jack-knife and a yoke for his oxen

3. What is the Saturday-night feeling?

   a. the satisfaction of sitting around a warm fire with a loving family

   b. the feeling of clean skin and clean clothes

   c. the feeling that all the chores are done well and we can relax

4. What three chores does Almanzo have to do after school each day?

   a. clean the barn stalls, feed fresh hay to the cows, feed the cats

   b. feed fresh hay to the cows, mend barnyard fences, feed the cats

   c. clean the barn stalls, water the livestock, help mother in the kitchen

5. Why does Father get up during cold winter nights to exercise the young cattle?

   a. The cattle need more food and movement during winter to stay healthy.

   b. They stand in the barn all winter and Father thinks they need the extra exercise.

   c. If the cattle lay still on a very cold night they might freeze in their sleep.

6. What unexpected news does Almanzo learn when he overhears his Father and Mr. Corse talking?

   a. The teacher who was seriously hurt by the Hardscrabble boys had been Mr. Corse's friend.

   b. Mr. Corse is an experienced boxer and isn't too worried about the bullies.

   c. The bullwhip Mr. Corse used to defeat the big boys belongs to his own father.

7. What type of weather is perfect for cutting ice? Why? **Both** parts of the answer must be correct!

   a. Extreme cold, because when the ice blocks are lifted from the pond they won't drip.

   b. A warm winter day, when the cross-saw handles can be held on both ends and the ice is then easier to cut.

   c. Extreme cold, because everyone is in a hurry to get the job done quickly and warm up.

8. What does Almanzo like **best** about Saturdays, and what does he like **least**? **Both** must be true!

    a. no school / knowing that tomorrow he has to sit still all day

    b. baking day / taking a bath

    c. fewer chores on Saturday / taking a bath

9. How does the Wilder family spend their Sunday afternoons?

    a. They sit quietly because it is supposed to be a day of rest.

    b. They visit friends or relatives if the weather is nice.

    c. They read the Bible and pop popcorn together.

10. How do Almanzo and Alice make the work of loading potatoes into baskets more fun?

    a. They recite their favorite poems to each other while they work.

    b. They take a break to stop and drink cider so they won't get too hot and tired.

    c. They race against each other to see who can fill a basket faster.

Answer the following questions in complete sentences.

1. What is the setting of *Farmer Boy*? Where and in what year does it take place? _____

_____

2. Briefly describe the "surprise" that occurs at school involving Big Bill's gang and Mr. Corse. _____

_____

_____

_____

3. How do the Wilders keep the ice frozen even in the hot summer months? _____

_____

_____

4. What is Almanzo's "splendid" idea concerning his calves, and why does it go wrong? _____

_____

_____

_____

5. Why doesn't Father trust Almanzo around the colts? What does he fear will happen? _____

_____

_____

_____

Farmer Boy Quiz 1

Chapters 1-10

Name _____

Date _____

Write the letter of the vocabulary word on the line in front of its definition.

1. __g__ walked with heavy feet
2. __c__ calmly; peacefully
3. __a__ waking
4. __e__ disrespectfully
5. __i__ smooth; slick
6. __b__ quickly; with spirit
7. __d__ small, short-handled ax
8. __f__ sleepy
9. __h__ bent to one side
10. __j__ scented

a. rousing
b. briskly
c. placidly
d. hatchet
e. impudently
f. drowsy
g. trudged
h. askew
i. sleek
j. aromatic

Match each name below with a character description.

Mother	Pierre and Louis	Frank	Father	Alice
Mr. Corse	Hardscrabble boys	Almanzo	Eliza Jane	Star and Bright

1. _____Eliza Jane_____ bossy; always knows what is best to do

2. _____Almanzo_____ just starting school; almost nine years old

3. _____Hardscrabble boys_____ big, rough boys; everyone is afraid of them

4. _____Star and Bright_____ young oxen in need of "breaking"

5. _____Mother_____ short, plump, and pretty; has blue eyes and brown hair

6. _____Alice_____ races with Almanzo to fill potato baskets for town

7. _____Frank_____ has a "store-boughten" cap that Almanzo admires

8. _____Mr. Corse_____ gentle, patient, and never whips little boys

9. _____Father_____ stern, but has eyes that often twinkle

10. _____Pierre and Louis_____ live in the woods and never have to go to school

1. Why does Almanzo's teacher stay with the Wilder family at their home?

    a. He is poor and has nowhere else to go.

    b. He likes their family the best of all the other families.

    c. Each family boards the teacher for two weeks, and it is the Wilders' turn.

2. What gifts does Almanzo receive from his parents for his birthday? **Both** must be true!

    a. a sled and warm, woolen mittens

    b. a small yoke for his ox calves and a sled

    c. a jack-knife and a yoke for his oxen

3. What is the Saturday-night feeling?

    a. the satisfaction of sitting around a warm fire with a loving family

    b. the feeling of clean skin and clean clothes

    c. the feeling that all the chores are done well and we can relax

4. What three chores does Almanzo have to do after school each day?

    a. clean the barn stalls, feed fresh hay to the cows, feed the cats

    b. feed fresh hay to the cows, mend barnyard fences, feed the cats

    c. clean the barn stalls, water the livestock, help mother in the kitchen

5. Why does Father get up during cold winter nights to exercise the young cattle?

    a. The cattle need more food and movement during winter to stay healthy.

    b. They stand in the barn all winter and Father thinks they need the extra exercise.

    c. If the cattle lay still on a very cold night they might freeze in their sleep.

6. What unexpected news does Almanzo learn when he overhears his Father and Mr. Corse talking?

    a. The teacher who was seriously hurt by the Hardscrabble boys had been Mr. Corse's friend.

    b. Mr. Corse is an experienced boxer and isn't too worried about the bullies.

    c. The bullwhip Mr. Corse used to defeat the big boys belongs to his own father.

7. What type of weather is perfect for cutting ice? Why? **Both** parts of the answer must be correct!

    a. Extreme cold, because when the ice blocks are lifted from the pond they won't drip.

    b. A warm winter day, when the cross-saw handles can be held on both ends and the ice is then easier to cut.

    c. Extreme cold, because everyone is in a hurry to get the job done quickly and warm up.

8. What does Almanzo like **best** about Saturdays, and what does he like **least**? **Both** must be true!

   a. no school / knowing that tomorrow he has to sit still all day

   (b.) baking day / taking a bath

   c. fewer chores on Saturday / taking a bath

9. How does the Wilder family spend their Sunday afternoons?

   (a.) They sit quietly because it is supposed to be a day of rest.

   b. They visit friends or relatives if the weather is nice.

   c. They read the Bible and pop popcorn together.

10. How do Almanzo and Alice make the work of loading potatoes into baskets more fun?

   a. They recite their favorite poems to each other while they work.

   b. They take a break to stop and drink cider so they won't get too hot and tired.

   (c.) They race against each other to see who can fill a basket faster.

Answer the following questions in complete sentences.

1. What is the setting of *Farmer Boy*? Where and in what year does it take place? ____ The story is set in the year 1866. The story takes place in New York state.

2. Briefly describe the "surprise" that occurs at school involving Big Bill's gang and Mr. Corse. _____

   Big Bill and his gang threaten the teacher, but Mr. Corse surprises and defeats them with a bullwhip.

3. How do the Wilders keep the ice frozen even in the hot summer months? _____

   They stack the blocks and pack them in sawdust in the ice-house.

4. What is Almanzo's "splendid" idea concerning his calves, and why does it go wrong? _____

   Almanzo decides to see if his team of calves can pull his sled with passengers on it because Star and Bright are behaving so well. He has forgotten to teach them to obey his commands while he is riding behind them. He finds this out after his sled crashes.

5. Why doesn't Father trust Almanzo around the colts? What does he fear will happen? _____

   Father knows that young, unbroken horses are easily spoiled. If a careless boy scares or strikes a colt it could make it difficult or impossible to train well later.

Farmer Boy Quiz 2

Chapters 11-20

Name _____

Date _____

Write the letter of the vocabulary word on the line in front of its definition.

1. _____ to hurry
2. _____ to waste time; to be slow
3. _____ grading period; semester
4. _____ sandy
5. _____ question
6. _____ to stop short and refuse to go on
7. _____ sections, rows
8. _____ firmly; severely
9. _____ crafty; clever
10. _____ spotted

a. inquiry
b. dawdle
c. balk
d. hustle
e. term
f. gritty
g. dappled
h. shrewd
i. swathes
j. sternly

Match each name below with a character description.

Almanzo	French Joe/Lazy John	Lucy	Starlight	Bess and Beauty
tin-peddler	butter-buyer	Father	Eliza Jane	horse-buyer

1. _____ from New York City; has nice clothes; everybody likes him

2. _____ Beauty's colt

3. _____ jolly traveling salesman who tells good stories

4. _____ Father's old, gentle work-horses

5. _____ throws the blacking brush, leaving a stain on the wall

6. _____ teaches Almanzo a better way to grow pumpkins

7. _____ refuses to feed good watermelon rinds to a pig

8. _____ works for Father when extra help is needed

9. _____ Almanzo's suckling pig

10. _____ city man; has a waxed mustache and pointed black beard

1. Why do the farmers hurry to plant their good seeds in the springtime?

    a. They want to have more time for all the other jobs that need to be done in spring.

    b. The seeds will have a good start in growing before they can be overtaken by weeds.

    c. They want the crops to be ready for harvesting by the middle of summer.

2. Why are the Wilders eager to see Nick Brown?

    a. He brings stories, songs, and news from his travels with him, along with all his tin ware.

    b. Mother is excited to bargain and get a good price for her butter.

    c. By this time of year, the family is in need of money from selling their young horses.

3. How does the thin strange dog help the Wilder family?

    a. He guards the sheep from being stolen during the night.

    b. He barks a warning so Father can chase away thieves.

    c. He protects them from possible thieves.

4. Why does Almanzo anxiously await the dark of the moon in May?

    a. It is time to plant crops, and he loves working in the fields with Father.

    b. It becomes warmer and he can stay outdoors longer.

    c. He can stay home from school and plant pumpkins.

5. On Independence Day, when Almanzo wants a nickel, why does Father ask him about potatoes?

    a. He wants him to understand how much work goes into earning money and to value it.

    b. Father wants to convince Almanzo not to buy lemonade.

    c. Father wants to impress his adult friend with Almanzo's farming knowledge.

6. What causes Almanzo to fall behind in his work during sheep-shearing?

    a. He is distracted by all the hay in the loft and begins to play in it.

    b. The experienced shearers work too quickly, and he is distracted by a cat and kittens.

    c. He is watching the shearers carefully so he can learn how to do it himself some day.

7. Why doesn't Almanzo ask his father to go fishing on a rainy day?

    a. He thinks his father will say it is wrong to waste time in idleness such as fishing.

    b. He doesn't really like to fish; he prefers to watch the colts in the meadow.

    c. He wants to stay at home where it is dry and help his mother and sisters with their indoor chores.

8. Why are the children in a frenzy on the last day before Mother and Father return from their trip?

    a. They have to fix the wallpaper in the parlor so their parents won't see the black mark.

    b. They have not done their chores and have to put the house in order before they arrive.

    c. They are afraid they will be punished for eating all the white sugar.

9. Why is summer haying-time Almanzo's favorite time of the year?

    a. He loves the long days when he can play in the hayloft and drink lemonade.

    b. He doesn't have to go to school in the summer!

    c. He loves the variety of the work and drinking fresh egg-nog.

10. Why is Father in a hurry to harvest the potatoes?

    a. He has so much other work to do for harvesting that is more important to get done.

    b. There is a threat of frost which would kill the potato crop.

    c. The family has no potatoes left to eat and they depend on them for food.

Answer the following questions in complete sentences.

1. In what small way does Father acknowledge that Almanzo is becoming more trustworthy around the young horses? _____

_____

2. Sheep-shearing is done as an assembly line. What is each person's job? _____

_____

_____

_____

3. Briefly describe what Father teaches Almanzo about growing pumpkins. _____

_____

_____

4. What happens between Almanzo and Eliza Jane in the parlor? _____

_____

_____

5. Explain why the perfect apples are picked, hauled, and stored very carefully. How re the imperfect apples used? _____

_____

_____

Farmer Boy Quiz 2

Chapters 11-20

Name _____

Date _____

Write the letter of the vocabulary word on the line in front of its definition.

1. __d__ to hurry
2. __b__ to waste time; to be slow
3. __e__ grading period; semester
4. __f__ sandy
5. __a__ question
6. __c__ to stop short and refuse to go on
7. __i__ sections, rows
8. __j__ firmly; severely
9. __h__ crafty; clever
10. __g__ spotted

a. inquiry
b. dawdle
c. balk
d. hustle
e. term
f. gritty
g. dappled
h. shrewd
i. swathes
j. sternly

Match each name below with a character description.

Almanzo	French Joe/Lazy John	Lucy	Starlight	Bess and Beauty
tin-peddler	butter-buyer	Father	Eliza Jane	horse-buyer

1. __butter-buyer__ — from New York City; has nice clothes; everybody likes him

2. __Starlight__ — Beauty's colt

3. __tin-peddler__ — jolly traveling salesman who tells good stories

4. __Bess and Beauty__ — Father's old, gentle work-horses

5. __Almanzo__ — throws the blacking brush, leaving a stain on the wall

6. __Father__ — teaches Almanzo a better way to grow pumpkins

7. __Eliza Jane__ — refuses to feed good watermelon rinds to a pig

8. __French Joe / Lazy John__ — works for Father when extra help is needed

9. __Lucy__ — Almanzo's suckling pig

10. __horse-buyer__ — city man; has a waxed mustache and pointed black beard

Choose the best answer for each question.

1. Why do the farmers hurry to plant their good seeds in the springtime?

    a. They want to have more time for all the other jobs that need to be done in spring.

    (b.) The seeds will have a good start in growing before they can be overtaken by weeds.

    c. They want the crops to be ready for harvesting by the middle of summer.

2. Why are the Wilders eager to see Nick Brown?

    (a.) He brings stories, songs, and news from his travels with him, along with all his tin ware.

    b. Mother is excited to bargain and get a good price for her butter.

    c. By this time of year, the family is in need of money from selling their young horses.

3. How does the thin strange dog help the Wilder family?

    a. He guards the sheep from being stolen during the night.

    b. He barks a warning so Father can chase away thieves.

    (c.) He protects them from possible thieves.

4. Why does Almanzo anxiously await the dark of the moon in May?

    a. It is time to plant crops, and he loves working in the fields with Father.

    b. It becomes warmer and he can stay outdoors longer.

    (c.) He can stay home from school and plant pumpkins.

5. On Independence Day, when Almanzo wants a nickel, why does Father ask him about potatoes?

    (a.) He wants him to understand how much work goes into earning money and to value it.

    b. Father wants to convince Almanzo not to buy lemonade.

    c. Father wants to impress his adult friend with Almanzo's farming knowledge.

6. What causes Almanzo to fall behind in his work during sheep-shearing?

    a. He is distracted by all the hay in the loft and begins to play in it.

    (b.) The experienced shearers work too quickly, and he is distracted by a cat and kittens.

    c. He is watching the shearers carefully so he can learn how to do it himself some day.

7. Why doesn't Almanzo ask his father to go fishing on a rainy day?

    (a.) He thinks his father will say it is wrong to waste time in idleness such as fishing.

    b. He doesn't really like to fish; he prefers to watch the colts in the meadow.

    c. He wants to stay at home where it is dry and help his mother and sisters with their indoor chores.

118   **Farmer Boy**   **Quiz 2**   **Chapters 11-20**

8. Why are the children in a frenzy on the last day before Mother and Father return from their trip?

    a. They have to fix the wallpaper in the parlor so their parents won't see the black mark.

    (b.) They have not done their chores and have to put the house in order before they arrive.

    c. They are afraid they will be punished for eating all the white sugar.

9. Why is summer haying-time Almanzo's favorite time of the year?

    a. He loves the long days when he can play in the hayloft and drink lemonade.

    b. He doesn't have to go to school in the summer!

    (c.) He loves the variety of the work and drinking fresh egg-nog.

10. Why is Father in a hurry to harvest the potatoes?

    a. He has so much other work to do for harvesting that is more important to get done.

    (b.) There is a threat of frost which would kill the potato crop.

    c. The family has no potatoes left to eat and they depend on them for food.

Answer the following questions in complete sentences.

---

1. In what small way does Father acknowledge that Almanzo is becoming more trustworthy around the young horses? Father allows him to help groom the four-year-old colts to get them ready for the horse-buyer.

2. Sheep-shearing is done as an assembly line. What is each person's job? Almanzo pushes each sheep through a gate. The men soap and rinse each one in the river. Then the sheep are herded to the river bank where the men help them out of the water.

3. Briefly describe what Father teaches Almanzo about growing pumpkins. He cuts a slit in the pumpkin vine and sticks a candle wick into it. The other end of the wick is placed in a pan of milk. The milk is wicked up into the vine and consumed by the growing pumpkin.

4. What happens between Almanzo and Eliza Jane in the parlor? Almanzo reacts against Eliza Jane's "bossing" and throws the stove polish brush at her, leaving a black stain on the parlor wallpaper. Later, Eliza Jane secretly patches the wallpaper to cover up for him.

5. Explain why the perfect apples are picked, hauled, and stored very carefully. How re the imperfect apples used? If an apple is bruised, it will rot, and the rot will spread to all of the apples; so one bad apple could spoil the entire crop. The imperfect apples are used to make cider.

Farmer Boy Quiz 3

Chapters 21-29

Name _____

Date _____

Write the letter of the vocabulary word on the line in front of its definition.

1. _____ flexible
2. _____ in a calming manner
3. _____ pointed
4. _____ one who works in return for instruction
5. _____ hard, outer covering of grain
6. _____ thankful
7. _____ trampled; worn down
8. _____ held tightly
9. _____ to polish by scrubbing
10. _____ scissors

a. trodden
b. clutched
c. tapered
d. scour
e. shears
f. apprentice
g. pliable
h. obliged
i. chaff
j. soothingly

Match each name below with a character description.

| Father | Mr. Thompson | Frank | Eliza Jane | the cobbler |
| Almanzo | Mr. Case | Alice | Mother | Mr. Paddock |

1. _____ suspicious of banks and selfish with his money

2. _____ gives up a warm baked potato because Almanzo is hurt

3. _____ gives Starlight to Almanzo to train

4. _____ feels that farming is more honorable than storekeeping

5. _____ would rather have a nimble sixpence than a slow shilling

6. _____ is mortified that Father drinks tea from his saucer

7. _____ wants to hire Almanzo as an apprentice

8. _____ wants to bring Starlight to the fair the following year

9. _____ the good-natured shoemaker

10. _____ urges Almanzo to disobey his father

1. What makes Almanzo feel grown-up and important at the fair?

   a. He is allowed to leave his parents and spend time playing with his cousin.

   b. He knows the names of all the different types of horses, cows, and sheep at the fair.

   c. He feels important talking about horses with Father.

2. Why does the bitter cold mean it is butchering-time?

   a. In the cold the meat will freeze quickly and stay frozen all winter.

   b. Some of the livestock always dies from the extremely cold temperatures and they don't want to waste the meat.

   c. There are fewer chores to do in winter, so Father has enough time to butcher.

3. Why don't the Wilders make their own shoes?

   a. They don't have the right quality of animal hide for shoes.

   b. Cobblers' work is highly skilled and requires special equipment.

   c. They are too busy farming and don't have time to make shoes.

4. Why does Father show Almanzo how to make the sled rather than just make it all for him?

   a. Father wants him to learn the skills by doing it himself, and he knows that will also teach him to more deeply appreciate and take care of the sled.

   b. Father doesn't have the time to make it for him; Almanzo has to help or it won't get done.

   c. He wants Almanzo to be able to fix his sled by himself if it is ever broken.

5. Describe how Almanzo feels while he spends time in the barn threshing and doing his chores.

   a. He dislikes being in the barn and would rather be out in the fresh outdoors.

   b. He feels good knowing he has helped with all the important work and can care for the animals.

   c. He enjoys working in the barn because it gives him a chance to see the horses often.

6. What does Frank want Almanzo to do at Christmas time? Does he do it?

   a. Frank wants him to hitch up the oxen team and go for a ride in the barnyard; Almanzo refuses.

   b. Frank encourages him to disobey Father and currycomb Starlight; Almanzo agrees.

   c. Frank wants Almanzo to climb into Starlight's stall and sit on her back; Almanzo refuses.

7. What is Almanzo's reaction when his mother wants him to stop work after his logging accident?

   a. He eats a bit more dinner to give him extra strength and takes a nap before returning to work.

   b. He is determined not to let a little accident stop him; he keeps working.

   c. He is so tired and sore that he agrees to stay home and let the others finish the logging.

8. What does Father mean when he tells Almanzo, "Learning is best put into practice"?

   a. Father means it's better to actually obey than to just talk about obeying.

   b. The saying means that learning something is better than practicing it.

   c. Father wants Almanzo to experience using his knowledge about math and the cost of hay by actually selling it himself in town.

9. Why does Father initially object to Almanzo taking the reward money from Mr. Thompson?

   a. Father believes that a person doesn't necessarily deserve a reward for common honesty.

   b. Father wants to secretly take the reward money and save it for Almanzo to have later.

   c. Father doesn't like Mr. Thompson and doesn't want Almanzo to be indebted to him.

10. What does Mr. Paddock discuss with Father?

   a. Mr. Paddock wants Almanzo to work for him as an apprentice.

   b. Mr. Paddock asks Father's permission to recommend Almanzo to another farmer for a job.

   c. Mr. Paddock admires Almanzo's honesty and wants to say so to Father.

Answer the following questions in complete sentences.

1. What does the threat of a switch have to do with Almanzo's good behavior before Christmas? ____

   _____

   _____

2. Give an example of how Almanzo has learned to use patience and gentleness in training his oxen.

   _____

   _____

3. Why is Almanzo so angry with Mr. Thompson? _____

   _____

   _____

4. Explain the difference between Mother's and Father's hopes for Almanzo's future. _____

   _____

   _____

   _____

5. What does Almanzo want more than anything in the world? How does he decide this? _____

   _____

   _____

   _____

Farmer Boy Quiz 3

Chapters 21-29

Name _____

Date _____

Write the letter of the vocabulary word on the line in front of its definition.

1. __g__ flexible
2. __j__ in a calming manner
3. __c__ pointed
4. __f__ one who works in return for instruction
5. __i__ hard, outer covering of grain
6. __h__ thankful
7. __a__ trampled; worn down
8. __b__ held tightly
9. __d__ to polish by scrubbing
10. __e__ scissors

a. trodden
b. clutched
c. tapered
d. scour
e. shears
f. apprentice
g. pliable
h. obliged
i. chaff
j. soothingly

Match each name below with a character description.

| Father | Mr. Thompson | Frank | Eliza Jane | the cobbler |
| Almanzo | Mr. Case | Alice | Mother | Mr. Paddock |

1. _____Mr. Thompson_____ suspicious of banks and selfish with his money

2. _____Alice_____ gives up a warm baked potato because Almanzo is hurt

3. _____Father_____ gives Starlight to Almanzo to train

4. _____Mother_____ feels that farming is more honorable than storekeeping

5. _____Mr. Case_____ would rather have a nimble sixpence than a slow shilling

6. _____Eliza Jane_____ is mortified that Father drinks tea from his saucer

7. _____Mr. Paddock_____ wants to hire Almanzo as an apprentice

8. _____Almanzo_____ wants to bring Starlight to the fair the following year

9. _____the cobbler_____ the good-natured shoemaker

10. _____Frank_____ urges Almanzo to disobey his father

1. What makes Almanzo feel grown-up and important at the fair?

    a. He is allowed to leave his parents and spend time playing with his cousin.

    b. He knows the names of all the different types of horses, cows, and sheep at the fair.

    c. He feels important talking about horses with Father.

2. Why does the bitter cold mean it is butchering-time?

    a. In the cold the meat will freeze quickly and stay frozen all winter.

    b. Some of the livestock always dies from the extremely cold temperatures and they don't want to waste the meat.

    c. There are fewer chores to do in winter, so Father has enough time to butcher.

3. Why don't the Wilders make their own shoes?

    a. They don't have the right quality of animal hide for shoes.

    b. Cobblers' work is highly skilled and requires special equipment.

    c. They are too busy farming and don't have time to make shoes.

4. Why does Father show Almanzo how to make the sled rather than just make it all for him?

    a. Father wants him to learn the skills by doing it himself, and he knows that will also teach him to more deeply appreciate and take care of the sled.

    b. Father doesn't have the time to make it for him; Almanzo has to help or it won't get done.

    c. He wants Almanzo to be able to fix his sled by himself if it is ever broken.

5. Describe how Almanzo feels while he spends time in the barn threshing and doing his chores.

    a. He dislikes being in the barn and would rather be out in the fresh outdoors.

    b. He feels good knowing he has helped with all the important work and can care for the animals.

    c. He enjoys working in the barn because it gives him a chance to see the horses often.

6. What does Frank want Almanzo to do at Christmas time? Does he do it?

    a. Frank wants him to hitch up the oxen team and go for a ride in the barnyard; Almanzo refuses.

    b. Frank encourages him to disobey Father and currycomb Starlight; Almanzo agrees.

    c. Frank wants Almanzo to climb into Starlight's stall and sit on her back; Almanzo refuses.

7. What is Almanzo's reaction when his mother wants him to stop work after his logging accident?

    a. He eats a bit more dinner to give him extra strength and takes a nap before returning to work.

    b. He is determined not to let a little accident stop him; he keeps working.

    c. He is so tired and sore that he agrees to stay home and let the others finish the logging.

8. What does Father mean when he tells Almanzo, "Learning is best put into practice"?

  a. Father means it's better to actually obey than to just talk about obeying.

  b. The saying means that learning something is better than practicing it.

  c. Father wants Almanzo to experience using his knowledge about math and the cost of hay by actually selling it himself in town.

9. Why does Father initially object to Almanzo taking the reward money from Mr. Thompson?

  a. Father believes that a person doesn't necessarily deserve a reward for common honesty.

  b. Father wants to secretly take the reward money and save it for Almanzo to have later.

  c. Father doesn't like Mr. Thompson and doesn't want Almanzo to be indebted to him.

10. What does Mr. Paddock discuss with Father?

  a. Mr. Paddock wants Almanzo to work for him as an apprentice.

  b. Mr. Paddock asks Father's permission to recommend Almanzo to another farmer for a job.

  c. Mr. Paddock admires Almanzo's honesty and wants to say so to Father.

Answer the following questions in complete sentences.

1. What does the threat of a switch have to do with Almanzo's good behavior before Christmas? ____

   Switches or a trip to the woodshed means the same thing: a spanking. Almanzo behaves well to avoid this.

2. Give an example of how Almanzo has learned to use patience and gentleness in training his oxen.

   When his team begins to see-saw, he takes Joe's advice and speaks to them gently to settle them and get them to pull together. He speaks encouragingly to them when they make mistakes.

3. Why is Almanzo so angry with Mr. Thompson? Almanzo is angry because Mr. Thompson called him a "durn boy" and implied that he was a thief.

4. Explain the difference between Mother's and Father's hopes for Almanzo's future. Mother feels working a town job will keep him dependent on others for his living and won't produce character in a man as farming would. Father wants to be sure Almanzo clearly understands his choices and he should make his own decision.

5. What does Almanzo want more than anything in the world? How does he decide this? _____

   He wants to be like Father, free and independent. He knows he doesn't want to live inside walls and please people he doesn't like. He wants to own horses, cows, and fields.

Farmer Boy
Final Test

Name _____

Date _____

Vocabulary: Write the letter of the vocabulary word next to its definition.

1. _____ crafty; clever   a. trudged
2. _____ calmly; peacefully   b. placidly
3. _____ to waste time; to be slow   c. briskly
4. _____ scented   d. aromatic
5. _____ question   e. shrewd
6. _____ flexible   f. inquiry
7. _____ walked with heavy feet   g. dawdle
8. _____ held tightly   h. tapered
9. _____ quickly; with spirit   i. pliable
10. _____ pointed   j. clutched

Character Identification: Choose the name that matches each description and write it on the line.

Father	tin-peddler	Frank	Almanzo	Mr. Thompson
Starlight	Pierre and Louis	Mother	Mr. Paddock	Eliza Jane

1. _____ short, plump, and pretty; has blue eyes and brown hair

2. _____ Beauty's colt

3. _____ live in the woods and never have to go to school

4. _____ a wheelwright; wants to hire Almanzo as an apprentice

5. _____ throws the blacking brush, leaving a stain on the wall

6. _____ jolly, traveling salesman that tells good stories

7. _____ bossy; always knows what is best to do

8. _____ stern, but has eyes that often twinkle

9. _____ urges Almanzo to disobey his father

10. _____ suspicious of banks and selfish with his money

Who Said That?: Match each name to a quotation and write the name on the line.

Mr. Corse	Mr. Paddock	Alice	Mother	Almanzo
Eliza Jane	Mr. Thompson	Father	tin-peddler	horse-buyer

1. _____ "I'll tell story for story and sing song for song ..."

2. _____ "You ever think of making a wheelwright out of him?"

3. _____ "When a man undertakes a job, he has to stick to it till he finishes it."

4. _____ "All right, two hundred it is. I'll lose money by it, but here you are."

5. _____ "Stay in at recess and learn it."

6. _____ "You mean to say we must keep all that money in the house overnight!"

7. _____ "Well, this durn boy didn't steal any of it."

8. _____ "I guess I know how to handle my own calves."

9. _____ "I guess I was aggravating. But I didn't mean it."

10. _____ "This one's yours because you're hurt ..."

Literary Terms: Identify each sentence by writing "A" for alliteration, "S" for simile, or "O" for onomatopoeia.

1. _____ Their white blossoms were like foam on the field.

2. _____ Alice and Almanzo carried pails full of pieces of potato.

3. _____ The fifes tooted and the flutes shrilled.

4. _____ He blubbered and begged.

5. _____ Then—BOOM!

6. _____ Quick as black lightning the lash circled and struck and coiled again.

7. _____ The cold was cruel.

8. _____ The drummer beat rat-a-tat-tat and rub-a-dub-dub on the drum.

9. _____ The dark hung like a mist over the field.

10. _____ The little pig was as white as a lamb, and she liked Almanzo.

1. Why does Almanzo's teacher stay with the Wilder family at their home?

    a. He is poor and has nowhere else to go.

    b. He likes their family the best of all the other families.

    c. Each family boards the teacher for two weeks, and it is the Wilders' turn.

2. What gifts does Almanzo receive from his parents for his birthday? **Both** must be true!

    a. a sled and warm, woolen mittens

    b. a small yoke for his ox calves and a sled

    c. a jack-knife and a yoke for his oxen

3. How does the Wilder family spend their Sunday afternoons?

    a. They sit quietly because it is supposed to be a day of rest.

    b. They visit friends or relatives if the weather is nice.

    c. They read the Bible and pop popcorn together.

4. Why does Almanzo anxiously await the dark of the moon in May?

    a. It is time to plant crops, and he loves working in the fields with Father.

    b. It becomes warmer and he can stay outdoors longer.

    c. He can stay home from school and plant pumpkins.

5. On Independence Day, when Almanzo wants a nickel, why does Father ask him about potatoes?

    a. Father wants Almanzo to understand how much work goes into earning money and to value it.

    b. Father wants to convince Almanzo not to buy lemonade.

    c. Father wants to impress his adult friend with Almanzo's farming knowledge.

6. Why is summer haying-time one of Almanzo's favorite times of the year?

    a. He loves the long days when he can play in the hayloft and drink lemonade.

    b. He doesn't have to go to school in the summer!

    c. He loves the variety of the work and drinking fresh egg-nog.

7. Why don't the Wilders make their own shoes?

    a. They don't have the right quality of animal hide for shoes.

    b. Cobblers' work is highly skilled and requires special equipment.

    c. They are too busy farming and don't have time to make shoes.

8. Why does Father show Almanzo how to make the sled rather than just make it all for him?

    a. Father wants him to learn the skills by doing it himself, and he knows that will also teach him to more deeply appreciate and take care of the sled.

    b. Father doesn't have the time to make it for him; Almanzo has to help or it won't get done.

    c. He wants Almanzo to be able to fix his sled by himself if it is ever broken.

9. Describe how Almanzo feels while he spends time in the barn threshing and doing his chores.

    a. He dislikes being in the barn and would rather be out in the fresh outdoors.

    b. He feels good knowing he has helped with all the important work and can care for the animals.

    c. He enjoys working in the barn because it gives him a chance to see the horses often.

10. What does Mr. Paddock discuss with Father?

    a. Mr. Paddock wants Almanzo to work for him as an apprentice.

    b. Mr. Paddock asks Father's permission to recommend Almanzo to another farmer for a job.

    c. Mr. Paddock admires Almanzo's honesty and wants to say so to Father.

Elements of Literature: Write a short phrase or sentence to answer each question.

1. What does the term "character" mean? _____

_____

2. Who is the main character in *Farmer Boy*? _____

_____

3. Describe the setting of *Farmer Boy*. _____

_____

_____

4. Tell what the term "plot" means in literature. _____

_____

_____

5. What is the **overall** plot of *Farmer Boy*? What one main thing does the whole book describe and

talk about? _____

_____

_____

_____

_____

1. Throughout most of the book, Father does not trust Almanzo around the colts. What does he fear will happen? _____

_____

2. Name and **briefly** describe TWO different salesmen that visit the Wilder farm. _____

_____

_____

_____

3. The Wilders grow or make much of what they use for everyday living. List three things they need on a regular basis that they produce themselves on their farm. _____

_____

_____

4. Choose one of the following "lessons" that Almanzo learns as a child, and give an example from the book of how he learned or used this lesson. *(patience, the value of money, telling the truth)*

_____

_____

_____

5. What does Father do at the end of the book that proves he thinks Almanzo is growing up? __

_____

Paragraph: 3-5 sentences

Describe a farmer based on what you know after reading *Farmer Boy.*

_____

_____

_____

_____

_____

_____

_____

Farmer Boy
Final Test

Name _____

Date _____

Vocabulary: Write the letter of the vocabulary word next to its definition.

1. __e__ crafty; clever
2. __b__ calmly; peacefully
3. __g__ to waste time; to be slow
4. __d__ scented
5. __f__ question
6. __i__ flexible
7. __a__ walked with heavy feet
8. __j__ held tightly
9. __c__ quickly; with spirit
10. __h__ pointed

a. trudged
b. placidly
c. briskly
d. aromatic
e. shrewd
f. inquiry
g. dawdle
h. tapered
i. pliable
j. clutched

Character Identification: Choose the name that matches each description and write it on the line.

| Father | tin-peddler | Frank | Almanzo | Mr. Thompson |
| Starlight | Pierre and Louis | Mother | Mr. Paddock | Eliza Jane |

1. ____Mother____ short, plump, and pretty; has blue eyes and brown hair

2. ____Starlight____ Beauty's colt

3. ____Pierre and Louis____ live in the woods and never have to go to school

4. ____Mr. Paddock____ a wheelwright; wants to hire Almanzo as an apprentice

5. ____Almanzo____ throws the blacking brush, leaving a stain on the wall

6. ____tin-peddler____ jolly, traveling salesman that tells good stories

7. ____Eliza Jane____ bossy; always knows what is best to do

8. ____Father____ stern, but has eyes that often twinkle

9. ____Frank____ urges Almanzo to disobey his father

10. ____Mr. Thompson____ suspicious of banks and selfish with his money

Who Said That?: Match each name to a quotation and write the name on the line.

Mr. Corse	Mr. Paddock	Alice	Mother	Almanzo
Eliza Jane	Mr. Thompson	Father	tin-peddler	horse-buyer

1. _____tin-peddler_____ "I'll tell story for story and sing song for song …"

2. _____Mr. Paddock_____ "You ever think of making a wheelwright out of him?"

3. _____Father_____ "When a man undertakes a job, he has to stick to it till he finishes it."

4. _____horse-buyer_____ "All right, two hundred it is. I'll lose money by it, but here you are."

5. _____Mr. Corse_____ "Stay in at recess and learn it."

6. _____Mother_____ "You mean to say we must keep all that money in the house overnight!"

7. _____Mr. Thompson_____ "Well, this durn boy didn't steal any of it."

8. _____Almanzo_____ "I guess I know how to handle my own calves."

9. _____Eliza Jane_____ "I guess I was aggravating. But I didn't mean it."

10. _____Alice_____ "This one's yours because you're hurt …"

Literary Terms: Identify each sentence by writing "A" for alliteration, "S" for simile, or "O" for onomatopoeia.

1. __S__ Their white blossoms were like foam on the field.

2. __A__ Alice and Almanzo carried pails full of pieces of potato.

3. __O__ The fifes tooted and the flutes shrilled.

4. __A__ He blubbered and begged.

5. __O__ Then—BOOM!

6. __S__ Quick as black lightning the lash circled and struck and coiled again.

7. __A__ The cold was cruel.

8. __O__ The drummer beat rat-a-tat-tat and rub-a-dub-dub on the drum.

9. __S__ The dark hung like a mist over the field.

10. __S__ The little pig was as white as a lamb, and she liked Almanzo.

1. Why does Almanzo's teacher stay with the Wilder family at their home?

    a. He is poor and has nowhere else to go.

    b. He likes their family the best of all the other families.

    (c.) Each family boards the teacher for two weeks, and it is the Wilders' turn.

2. What gifts does Almanzo receive from his parents for his birthday? **Both** must be true!

    a. a sled and warm, woolen mittens

    (b.) a small yoke for his ox calves and a sled

    c. a jack-knife and a yoke for his oxen

3. How does the Wilder family spend their Sunday afternoons?

    (a.) They sit quietly because it is supposed to be a day of rest.

    b. They visit friends or relatives if the weather is nice.

    c. They read the Bible and pop popcorn together.

4. Why does Almanzo anxiously await the dark of the moon in May?

    a. It is time to plant crops, and he loves working in the fields with Father.

    b. It becomes warmer and he can stay outdoors longer.

    (c.) He can stay home from school and plant pumpkins.

5. On Independence Day, when Almanzo wants a nickel, why does Father ask him about potatoes?

    (a.) Father wants Almanzo to understand how much work goes into earning money and to value it.

    b. Father wants to convince Almanzo not to buy lemonade.

    c. Father wants to impress his adult friend with Almanzo's farming knowledge.

6. Why is summer haying-time one of Almanzo's favorite times of the year?

    a. He loves the long days when he can play in the hayloft and drink lemonade.

    b. He doesn't have to go to school in the summer!

    (c.) He loves the variety of the work and drinking fresh egg-nog.

7. Why don't the Wilders make their own shoes?

    a. They don't have the right quality of animal hide for shoes.

    (b.) Cobblers' work is highly skilled and requires special equipment.

    c. They are too busy farming and don't have time to make shoes.

8. Why does Father show Almanzo how to make the sled rather than just make it all for him?

   (a.) Father wants him to learn the skills by doing it himself, and he knows that will also teach him to more deeply appreciate and take care of the sled.

   b. Father doesn't have the time to make it for him; Almanzo has to help or it won't get done.

   c. He wants Almanzo to be able to fix his sled by himself if it is ever broken.

9. Describe how Almanzo feels while he spends time in the barn threshing and doing his chores.

   a. He dislikes being in the barn and would rather be out in the fresh outdoors.

   (b.) He feels good knowing he has helped with all the important work and can care for the animals.

   c. He enjoys working in the barn because it gives him a chance to see the horses often.

10. What does Mr. Paddock discuss with Father?

   (a.) Mr. Paddock wants Almanzo to work for him as an apprentice.

   b. Mr. Paddock asks Father's permission to recommend Almanzo to another farmer for a job.

   c. Mr. Paddock admires Almanzo's honesty and wants to say so to Father.

Elements of Literature: Write a short phrase or sentence to answer each question.

1. What does the term "character" mean?

   Character means who the story is about.

2. Who is the main character in *Farmer Boy*?

   Almanzo (James) Wilder

3. Describe the setting of *Farmer Boy*.

   The story is set in 1866, on a farm in New York state.

4. Tell what the term "plot" means in literature.

   Plot means action or what happens in the story.

5. What is the **overall** plot of *Farmer Boy*? What one main thing does the whole book describe and

   talk about?   The overall plot is about the childhood events and lessons of Almanzo Wilder.

Short Answer: Write a phrase or sentence for each question.

1. Throughout most of the book, Father does not trust Almanzo around the colts. What does he fear will happen? _____ He knows that a young boy can easily do something that will spoil a colt, thus making them more difficult or impossible to train later.

2. Name and **briefly** describe TWO different salesmen that visit the Wilder farm. _____

   Possible answers include the tin-peddler, the horse-buyer, the butter-buyer, or the cobbler.

   _____

   _____

3. The Wilders grow or make much of what they use for everyday living. List three things they need on a regular basis that they produce themselves on their farm. _____ Answers may include wool for cloth, other items of clothing, butter, most of their meat, vegetables and grain, candles, soap, sleds, some tools (i.e., flail), ice, and wood for heat and building.

4. Choose one of the following "lessons" that Almanzo learns as a child, and give an example from the book of how he learned or used this lesson. *(patience, the value of money, telling the truth)*

   Answers may include: **patience** - training the oxen, waiting to train the colt

   value of money - 50¢ on Independence Day, growing potatoes, buying the pig

   telling the truth - his milk-fed pumpkin, asking for money, Mr. Thompson's pocketbook

5. What does Father do at the end of the book that proves he thinks Almanzo is growing up? _____

   He tells Almanzo he can have Starlight for his own to train.

Paragraph: 3-5 sentences

Describe a farmer based on what you know after reading *Farmer Boy*.

   Answers will vary.

   _____

   _____

   _____

   _____

   _____

   _____